Measure

A REVIEW OF FORMAL POETRY

VOLUME 11, ISSUE 2
2016

EDITORS
ROB GRIFFITH
PAUL BONE

ASSOCIATE EDITOR
KATIE DARBY MULLINS

CONTRIBUTING EDITOR
WILLIAM BAER

ADMINISTRATIVE ASSISTANT
KATHY MARTYN

ADVISORY BOARD
RHINA P. ESPAILLAT
DANA GIOIA
MICHAEL HEFFERNAN
MARK JARMAN
CARRIE JERRELL
DAVID MIDDLETON
WYATT PRUNTY
TIMOTHY STEELE

INTERNS
NEIL BROOKHOUSE
SARAH BUTLER
BETH BRUNMEIER
OLI ROSS-MUSICK

EDITORIAL OFFICE

Measure: A Review of Formal Poetry
Department of Creative Writing
University of Evansville
1800 Lincoln Avenue
Evansville, IN 47722

PUBLICATION

Measure: A Review of Formal Poetry is published twice each year.

SUBSCRIPTIONS

One-year subscriptions (2 issues) are $18, two-year subscriptions (4 issues) are $34, and three-year subscriptions (6 issues) are $50. Current and back issues are available for $15 each at our website.

SUBMISSIONS

Please see our website for complete submission guidelines.

WEBSITE

measurepress.com/measure/

SUPPORT

Funding for *Measure* is provided by a generous grant from the Ball Brothers Foundation of Muncie, from the Venture Fund, a program administered by the Independent Colleges of Indiana (ICI) for the benefit of Indiana's independent colleges and universities. Additional funding and support is provided by the University of Evansville. We would like to express our sincere appreciation to both organizations without whom this publication would not be possible.

ISSN

1555-4791

ISBN-10

1-939574-24-2

ISBN-13

978-1-939574-24-4

Contents

The Air Plant	Mark Jarman	1
Days or Light Years Ahead	Mark Jarman	3
End of the Day. Knifing Wind.	Mark Jarman	4
No One Understood the Final Meal	Mark Jarman	5
Variations on a Theme by Martial	Charles Martin	6
Two Philosophical Sonnets	Tony Barnstone	9
John Singer Sargent: The Black Brook	Roy Scheele	11
Andrew Wyeth: Christina's World	Roy Scheele	12
Absence	Leslie Monsour	13
The Minx	Arthur Rimbaud	
(Translated by A.M. Juster)		14
Mouth	Bruce Bond	15
Confession	Bruce Bond	16
The Book of Kings	James Matthew Wilson	17
A Final Note	Jeff Hardin	20
Embraced	Mike Alexander	21
Tech Support	Gilbert Allen	23
THE 2016 X.J. KENNEDY PARODY AWARD		
Judge's Note	A.M. Juster	24
Archaic Torso of Barbie	Robert Schechter	26
Now Hear This	Mae Scanlan	27
Swim-Fever	John Ridland	28
from *The Fortunes of Poetry in an Age of Unmaking*	James Matthew Wilson	29
The Archaeology of Grief	Ashley Anna McHugh	50
Girl Found Dead in the Sequatchie Valley	Chad Abushanab	51
Tabu	Moira Egan	53
The New World	Sofia M. Starnes	54
Directions	Dolores Stewart	56
Salt Memories	Kathryn Jacobs	57
Muse	James Haines	58
Green Lights	Thom Satterlee	59
Mr Larkin on Photography	N.S. Thompson	60
Fence Building	Stephen Scaer	62
Mad to be Saved	Stephen Bluestone	63
Nostalgia Piece	Peter Cooley	64
End Times	Quincy R. Lehr	65
He Waited for Days	Allison Adair	66
Lymphoma	Allison Adair	67
Tomato Vines	Dan Campion	69

Sam and Andre	Simon Hunt	70
A Madwoman	Jeff Holt	72
You Outweigh Me	Rob Jackson	73
On Patrol	Bill Glose	75
Psalm: & they shall smoke	Billy Reynolds	76
Ode I.11		
(Translated by David W. Landrum)	Horace	78
Another Art	John Ridland	79
Agamemnon's Return	John Ridland	80
Sleeping Bear	Stephen Palos	81
Chiaroscuro	Herb Wahlsteen	82
Lost Daughters	Gail White	85
Ariel Released	Richard Widerkehr	86
Sunflowers	Katherine Smith	88
One Death	Susan McLean	89
Everness	Terese Coe	90
For My Wife, Late Summer, Gardening	Robert McNamara	91
Anthracite	Catherine Chandler	92
What We See	Stuart Jay Silverman	93
A Brief History of the World in Two Parts	Stuart Jay Silverman	94
Acquiesce (I)	Kim Bridgford	96
The Tate Gallery Ophelia	Stephen Gibson	97
Ophelia	Stephen Gibson	98
Drought	Burt Myers	99

BOOK REPRINTS

The Neighbors Upstairs	Michael Shewmaker	100
The Illusionist	Michael Shewmaker	101
School Bus Graveyard	Michael Shewmaker	102
This is the Neighbor Kid Who Killed the Cat	Cody Walker	103
We Hated Our Lives	Cody Walker	104
Conditional	Cody Walker	105
Ornament	Anna Lena Phillips Bell	106
Bonaparte Crossing the Rhine	Anna Lena Phillips Bell	108
Green Man	Anna Lena Phillips Bell	109

ACKNOWLEDGMENTS	110
CONTRIBUTORS	111
THE 2017 X.J. KENNEDY PARODY AWARD	119
THE 2017 HOWARD NEMEROV SONNET AWARD	120

MARK JARMAN

The Air Plant

He sat across from me once, confessing crimes,
money paid him under the table, sitting birds
bagged driving home from work. But were they crimes?
All I could hear were humanizing words. . . .

This grandfather who always had a garden,
did all the cooking for his second wife,
sold cars, sat quietly to the side
at family things, and lived the longest life.

He pointed to a plant tacked to a post
of his lanai, and said it lived on air.
It looked uprooted, a weed scalped and displayed,
but also as if it would flourish there.

He grew the lantana for Ana's hummingbirds.
He put my hand on the ironbark eucalyptus.
The garden was his alone, even a grandchild
was admitted there by special permission.

His handshake stirred your hand from side to side.
He greeted friends in public, "You old stinker!"
He dug up an enormous cactus root,
a hundred pound white plug. And I, the little thinker,

with no idea of what thinking was worth,
watched without offering help, while asking questions.
Barechested, tanned and silvery, grunting and focused,
he rocked the root back and forth in the soaked earth.

These images of him hang in the air. He would page through
a coffee table book on Christmas day,
or go outside at Easter to cut flowers,
away from noise of children, family.

Two wives, a child with each of them, a long
retirement in the San Fernando Valley,
hands that were meant to be a surgeon's,
turned to making money, the work of engines.

Or was the story of his med school hopes
only a story that the family told
and hung like a diploma on his past?
He never mentioned it. The tale grew cold.

But it's from him a name comes from the trees,
Caledonian pines and oaken forests,
faring through centuries of leaf shadow,
shedding a single consonant and vowel.

And what was wild weeded, domesticated,
Forester stripped out inside to *Foster*,
with the green touch, though never mine, intact,
sparking the seed, setting the plant in air.

And from him all that I think I take
is my middle name, part of my mother's small dowry,
and nothing else I can identify
except a need to know birds, flowers, and trees.

MARK JARMAN

Days or Light Years Ahead

Days or light years ahead,
as Jacques Lacan has said,
a letter always arrives
at its destination.

Even a dead letter,
a message in dimpled clay,
its data fossilized,
arrives, all the better

for us to crack its codes —
news from the front,
fresh odes,
old news from lover to lover.

Folded in wave or particle,
envelope, river bed,
a letter arrives, is always arriving
at its fate — to be read or unread.

MARK JARMAN

End of the Day. Knifing Wind.

End of the day. Knifing wind.
Slanting twilight like melon rind.
Prickling sleet. Brisk afterglow.
To go home or not to go.

And morning then. Taste on the tongue
of last night's thirst, a dream sprung
like a tricky murderer from jail.
A spray of sunshine. Gunshot hail.

The night between. After the day,
at either end, a mind astray
among bare crowns and roots of trees,
touching the raw extremities.

End of dawn. And the night's end,
with headlights sweeping around the bend,
catching one afraid to balk
with deer blind eyes, and forward walk.

MARK JARMAN

No One Understood the Final Meal

No one understood the final meal,
that it was final, each part with a meaning.
No one understood, as it was served —
Each portion of the body poured, doled out.

Strange flesh. Strange drink.
Each portion of his body.
And as they ate and drank, he talked,
even had a private conversation.

All they remembered was eating with their friend,
a meal they'd had so many times
and known the order of. What was the order?
But who can remember dinner yesterday?

Forgiven for a crime not yet committed,
enjoined to remember someone not yet lost,
they tried to bring them back —
the taste and texture, somehow, the meal, him.

CHARLES MARTIN

Variations On A Theme By Martial

for X.J. Kennedy

Faenius, grieving, consecrates the grove
And field surrounding this new sepulcher
To Antulla, whom he will always love.
Their daughter's parents will rejoin her here
In this dear place. If you would have it, know
That those it serves will never let it go.
— Epigrams, *Book I, cxvi*

1.
A Christian, as it happened. No, his wife,
But under torture, he confessed, to spare
Their pretty son. We let him buy that life
By making the Emperor his only heir.
Boy's in a Spanish mine. His parents made
A brilliant show on Nero's promenade.

2.
The fortune that I spent to entertain
That imbecile reclining at my table
("More peacock tongue? Do try the monkey brain...")
Came back as the bad penny in the fable:
Five worthless acres in the Sabine Hills.
His "gift" to me. How will I pay my bills?

3.
A madman who came here by accident
And without any other place to go,
Shared quarters with the tomb's sole resident

Until he starved to death? Perhaps, although
I have another thought: they say the one
Who built this for his daughter had a son…

4.
Alaric wants the vineyard where the slope's
A little less uneven. Let's begin
With clearing off the field. Right in that copse,
There's an old tomb whose roof has fallen in.
Sure, it's been looted — but just keep in mind
I get a cut of anything you find.

5.
Each died of wounds inflicted by the other
At nearly the same time: and who knows whether
The two of them cried out to the same mother,
Were strangers or old foes who'd come together
Briefly to let a trial by arms decide
Between them for a plot of land, a bride?

6.
The topmost layer is a neat, long row
Of hostages, brought here in trucks and vans
Along the dirt road from the town below,
After an action by the partisans.
Machine gun bullets scarred the low stone wall.
We haven't gone down very far at all.

7.
We live upon the surface, as did they.
What lies below, is largely unexplored;
Old stuff that only gets in our way
Is best forgotten, or at least ignored,
As we make our way around a fertile star
On our inheritance, this abattoir.

8.
My cousin'll take care of it for you,
And I can promise it'll cost much less
Than months without your licenses would do.
Da Faenio's expanding! You don't need stress,
You need a newer, larger parking lot,
So let the dead bury the dead — or not!

TONY BARNSTONE

Two Philosophical Sonnets

Camera Obscura

Descartes installed the eyeball of an ox
in a small hole through which the daylight sprayed
inverted figures of the world's parade
on a white screen in a closed room's dark box,

like your idea of me, an image thrown
on the back wall of your dark skull. You face
the page. I face the backside of your face.
I wander lost, but I am not alone

inside your head. Something stalks this house
with walls of blue-veined flesh, with ancient casements
shuttered like eyes, the iron door a mouth
that opens on the dreadful secret basement.

Which one of us lies dreaming darkly there?
Who's at the top, one foot upon the stair?

The Prisoner

She woke up with her head and body chained
so tight she couldn't move or turn her neck.
Before her on a screen the grey planes flamed
and heroes wrestled villains on the deck.

Later, the actors, nude, enacted passion,
and everything was conflict, action, friction
resolved in half an hour in the fashion
of life converted into flashing fiction.

Behind her must have been a film projector
that cast the blaze and shadow for her eyes,
but she couldn't turn to see the show's director,
so she sat there filling up with lies

about a heroine who slips the chain,
unlocks the iron door, escapes her brain.

Roy Scheele

John Singer Sargent:
The Black Brook

(oil on canvas, ca. 1908)

Part of it is in shade, and part in sun.
So is the woman sitting at its edge,
her hands around one knee, her skirt in white
(or cream perhaps), upper sleeves and torso
a sort of gray or tan, her eyes cast down
to where the water trails away in light
in her abstracted gaze. She could reach out
and touch the yellow flowers to her left,
but she no longer sees them. Sunlight lays
its own reflection on the current here,
the water purling over darkened stone —
its little song accompanies her thought.
As each gleam rides in place, her listening,
besides the sound, takes in the glistening.

ROY SCHEELE

Andrew Wyeth: Christina's World

(tempera on panel, 1948)

The focal point is her own struggle here.
But to the right above her on the hill,
an item of dark clothing fidgets still
between the ell and an outlying shed,
its every wriggle in the breeze a blur.
Her own dress, pink and faded, without frill,
holds steady with her as she drinks her fill
of that quick movement dancing in her stead.
Her dead-gray hands claw at the pasture grass,
but the steep, tumbling slope won't let her pass.
Even the few worn ruts can make their way
all on their own, and the birds above her
swerving into the barn — what is there to say?
Only the sky, it seems, is left to love her.

LESLIE MONSOUR

Absence

Today the sparrows sound a bit more formal,
As if they had some tribute to declare;
Wild honeybees imbibe the bright oxalis
And sip the rosemary with gentler care.

A warming softness settles through the garden;
Its sweet lament lingers in every shape.
There's nothing here that will not miss her presence
And nothing that her presence can escape.

ARTHUR RIMBAUD

The Minx

In the paneled dining room, imbued
With fruit and varnish, I, without a care,
Pick a plate of dicey Belgian food
And amuse myself in my huge chair.

I hear the clock while eating, glad and shy.
Kitchen doors blow open with a gust
— Then this servant blows in (I don't know why)
Kerchief loose, hairdo coyly mussed.

And as her quaking pinkie slides down
Her pale orange-pink cheek of velvet down
While she's pouting like a three-year-old,

Tight in to lull me, she put plates out
— Then, like *that* (to get a kiss, no doubt)
Whispers, "Feel right *here*: my cheek is cold…"

Translated by A.M. Juster

BRUCE BOND

Mouth

Once you cupped the wick
lit with a surge of milk,
and as you grew, hunger
grew, and as you sighed,
made large by desires
that made me small, the *O*
from which I first drank
bound me to its absence.
Even now I go weak
against the warmth of bodies
that are not there, and yet
I relish my appetite
for what it cannot fill,
how it, like blood, persists,
less as meaningful
than filled with the purpose
meaning longs to possess.
If only I could cut light
into small and smaller
morsels. To speak this way
showers me with pins
and angels beyond number.
The archer knows, poised
to split the sweet spot:
the tinier the better,
the deeper the attraction
that focuses the needle.
Sweet red dwarf star, sweet heart
of the target, sweet pistil
of the rose whose petals
ripple outward. Like a cry.

Bruce Bond

Confession

I knew a boy who apologized so often
his voice began to dominate the conversation.

His heart was a damaged doll with a string
to make it talk without a heartbeat. Only string.

I too was broken and saw my brokenness in him
whom I avoided. I'm sorry, I told him, time

and time again, in the dollhouse of my head.
Some days a doll gave my apologies instead.

Dear boy, I asked, if guilt is the nail, is fear
the hammer. Are you there, dear. Are you still there.

Are you the sun in the dollhouse of the moon: you,
who speaks when spoken, who listens, child, when listened to.

James Matthew Wilson

The Book of Kings

"Is that how you met Dave?" she asked. "I mean,
Some men's group for the recently divorced?"
   They were at dinner. "No, way after that,"
Bresson said, "He'd moved on long since, I guess;
In fact, the way he talked, you'd think he was
One of those bachelor types who hop from girl
To girl with no excuse besides the season's
Changed." "Right," she said, and took a drink, then dabbed
Her lips with the cloth napkin, smoothed it out,
And spread it once again upon her lap.
   He'd noticed when she came in how her hips
Pressed tight against her skirt; her legs were lean
And pale and made him think of the word "flesh."
And now, he thought, she's interested: she knows
The wine might stain her teeth.
                          She smiled, then said,
"If you'd known him before, his wife, Michelle,
You wouldn't believe it — how he's changed, how he
Could put so much into someone, and now . . ."
   "Now, not," he said.
                          "When things were near the end,
He'd brought in some new client: I won't say
The name. You'd know it. Big. And, well, Michelle
Comes home from work to find him dancing, there,
Just dancing — you know, right out on the driveway,
His shirt flaps hanging out, his collar open.
She'd always known he loved her — so devoted,
I mean, she'd almost stayed with him because
She couldn't understand it and felt bad
She couldn't give it back." Bresson jumped in,
"Now, not," he said again, "not him."

                                            "He looked,
Prancing out in the drive, not loving but
Pathetic. Three weeks later, she moved out,
Left him the house. She couldn't *look* at him."
    He'd booked the table, and the movie she
Had picked up tickets for would start at ten.
Plenty of time to linger and fill in
The privacy that muzak wrapped around them
With just that sort of talk one wouldn't risk
On a first date — not normally, at least,
But *maybe* if it had been set up by
One's balding colleague, the roving divorcé.
    Bresson had heard the show was straight up gore,
Two hours of blood and screaming; she insisted
Reviewers called it brooding and suspenseful.
But either way, between that odd choice and
The second bottle of the Chateauneuf-
Du Pape he'd ordered when she didn't shake
Her head immediately, it seemed to him
That either they were comfortable together
Because they were *together* (and so, Dave,
Whom Bresson knew just from the club, and whose
Life seemed a wild, not-quite-sordid, string
Of stories about women, had been right),
Or just because, when the film ended, they
Would never be again. He filled her glass.
    The salad on his plate was mostly gone,
A few dark sprigs, brown beads of vinegar
Stranded in oil. Beyond its glassy front,
He saw the restaurant's lights, gleaming on slick
Macadam, and the traffic headed south
Slowed by the rain with wipers beating, furiously.
    "One time I went out with his ex. Michelle,
I mean. They'd settled the divorce, and she
Was trying to hold onto as many friendships

As possible. Most people blamed her, then;
And, well, okay, I thought, if he's pathetic,
You had to know that going in. To me
He seemed a little awkward, that was all.
He told dumb jokes, but I don't know a single
Guy in our office who could tell a good one."
Bresson sat mute, afraid to prove her point.

 "In any case, she tells me, one night, after
The separation, she'd come home — I guess
Real late. Perhaps she'd been out with a man;
She didn't say. I mean, she didn't want to.
She took her dress off, left it on the floor,
And went to wash her face. She might've been
In there five minutes. When she comes back out —
My God — she finds him standing there, right in
Her bedroom, holding that red dress, it all
Throttled and twisted, wrapped around his fists.
He looked at her awhile, and that was it."

 "He *left*, you mean?"

       "She said it looked as if
He wanted to say something or do something,
But just — you know — as if to show he could."

JEFF HARDIN

A Final Note

to Jill McCorkle

A broken beauty — this watching people sing
together, crowded close so harmonies
become more intimate — but I'll take it,
sit in a corner, trying not to weep.

The necks of guitars almost touching seems
appropriate to what the mournful words
are asking us. How long the final note
desires to live
                  our bones will not concede.

I see you leaning forward from your chair
across the room, regard me with a kindness,
as if to say you understand how rare
communion is of any kind, yet here

we are — and the moon is not the only light
we see, the land not dark, the stars unfallen.

MIKE ALEXANDER

Embraced

for Reardon

Thirty years ago, you wore that smirk
        that said the class was giant steps behind
                your syllabus, & always, thrift-store vests,
your signature attire. A poet's mind,
        you taught us by example, never rests.
                You'd talk about what makes a poet work.

Each lunch time, a Symposium. You'd talk
        of scaffolding in Chaucer or James Joyce
                with gravitas, then deftly explicate
Leon Trotsky in your Monty-Python voice.
        What bardos you'd be able to create
                once you were free of lesson plan & chalk.

You graduated. Free at last to do
        whatever you desired with your knowledge,
                you moved into an Artist Housing loft
in Paterson, & taught there at the college;
        nice gig, if tenure didn't make you soft.
                Old teachers only asked for news of you.

Retired teachers asked. In truth, the news
        was troubling. Too few particulars,
                too many mysteries. You disappeared
into an underworld of red brick bars,
        where wasted regulars you knew & feared
                offered you shots that you could not refuse.

Like Yeats' Raftery, you'd wax & wane;
        the phases of the moon. You'd celebrate
                two weeks without a drop, then wake outside,
sick, soiled, sorry, frothing-mad with hate
        at seeing your reflection, stripped of pride,
                your restless mind, an instrument of pain.

What then is left to say? – you went too soon,
        not soon enough? Forgive me if today
                I argue for a loss that makes no sense.
I see you smirking at me now, & pray
        that you, in one last Li Po reference,
                embraced yourself as you embraced the moon.

GILBERT ALLEN

Tech Support

Yellowstone, May 2015

We've stopped for geysers and the good Flush Ts.
You can't get any wireless out here
but Barbara thumbs her TracPhone, hopefully.
A solitary bison soon appears,

eating his way toward the parking lot.
Parched grass leads him to INFORMATION STATION
and its punctuating arrow — not
an inch between his rump and the pointing sign.

His shaggy head is shaking No No No.
He's strictly analog, and not IT.

Inevitable brown, descending, slow.

At least he doesn't say, "Reboot and see
if that corrects your problem. Good luck. *Ciao*."

I think we've been reduced to postcards now.

A.M. JUSTER

The 2016 X.J. Kennedy Parody Award

The first step in writing a poem parody is to find a striking poem, preferably a familiar one. That task becomes more challenging because contemporary poets have largely abandoned techniques that help us remember poetry. Accordingly, it is natural that poets tend to parody classic poems that are at least fifty years old, particularly "The Love Song of J. Alfred Prufrock" and "Do Not Go Gentle Into That Good Night." A brave soul who parodied a poem from Richard Wilbur's *Anterooms* navigated alone into recent waters.

The second step is to write a well-executed poem. Most, but not all, of the submissions parodied formal poems, so the usual considerations about not forcing rhyme and meter apply — unless the poet does it intentionally and well for humorous effect.

The third step is where many well-crafted submissions dropped out. A good parody should have something to say as a poem and not just inject funny words for giggles into the framework of the original.

For whatever these standards are worth, my plodding application of them left me with seven superior poems. The first two that I eliminated were noteworthy for their choice of poem. One poet used familiar Hammerstein & Kern lyrics to make a point I often make and the other offered bilingual takes on a difficult Robert Burns poem. I was also tempted by two clever riffs on Shakespearean sonnets — one in a chicken's voice and the other lamenting the rise of the e-book reader.

Among the remaining three, the competition was close. The poet who parodied "Sea-fever" struck a sentimental chord with me because the entry parodied the first poem I ever memorized; I tried to compensate for my sentimentality as best I could. Nonetheless, the parallelism between John Masefield's romanticized longing for the sailor's life and the parodist's wish to go swimming at the Y is clever, and it opened up an opportunity for cohesive humor in the parody.

Despite my longstanding maleness, the two parodies that spoke the most to me both had feminist inclinations. "Now Hear This" is a twist on a poem at the edge of the canon, Christina Rossetti's melancholy "When I am dead, my dearest." The parodist transforms the melodramatically dying poet's attempt to comfort her imminently widowed husband; in his or her hands it becomes a caustic criticism of a blithering husband by a wife going deaf, apparently blessedly so. The one-letter substitution in the first line is a stroke of genius, and the poem skillfully mimics Rossetti's tricky mix of trimeter and tetrameter.

The poem that I feel is most worthy of carrying the name of my friend and mentor, the great X.J. Kennedy, is "Archaic Torso of Barbie." It would not have occurred to me to parody the iconic "Archaic Torso of Apollo," but Rilke's poem is so familiar to poets, at least in translation, that it provides ample material for parody. As with the two finalists, I resonated to the parallel in subject matters between the original poem and its evil twin.

The rhyme and meter of "Barbie" is flawless, and the rhyme scheme exactly duplicates the rhyme scheme of the original poem; the poet even duplicated the enjambed phrase that extends into Rilke's fifth line. Impressively, the parodist's internal *bump/harrumph* off-rhyme in lines 6 and 7 echoes the *blenden/Lenden* in the same lines of Rilke. Most lines in the parody mirror in some way the content of lines in the original sonnet. In line 14, for instance, Apollo is blind, whereas in the parody Barbie is winking. That winking sets up the wickedest punchline of all the entries when Rilke's famous injunction "You must change your life" becomes a mischievous "You must change your toys."

It was a marvelous group of poems to read, and I was honored to decide something in Joe Kennedy's name.

ROBERT SCHECHTER

Archaic Torso of Barbie

We cannot know the famous plastic face
in which her eyes once swiveled. Still we find
her headless body's not exactly blind
but seems to peek out from the flimsy lace

in which some girl once dressed her. It's a fact.
Or else her bosom's bump would have no charm
and you would not harrumph with such alarm
to note the parts her nether regions lacked.

Or else you would not find it so aesthetic
to contemplate what plainly is synthetic
as if it were a creature that is real,

with all a living creature's woes and joys.
Or else you would not see her sex appeal.
She's winking at you. You must change your toys.

MAE SCANLAN

Now Hear This

When I am deaf, my dearest,
I shall not hear your rants
About the state of politics,
And what is wrong with France.

I shall not hear your petty jibes
About your brother Clarence,
Nor all your lengthy diatribes
Against my sainted parents.

I shall not hear your frequent puns
That often make no sense,
Expressly those unfunny ones
You make at my expense.

When push comes 'round to shove, dear mate,
I'll find you more endearing
And easier to tolerate
When I have lost my hearing.

JOHN RIDLAND

Swim-Fever

After John Masefield, "Sea-Fever"

I must go down to the gym to swim, to the crowded pool at the Y,
And all I ask is a half-lane and a clock to pace me by,
And the kick-board and the swim-fins and the white water shaking,
And a pull-buoy between my thighs and an age-group record breaking.

I must go down to the gym to swim, for the call of the swimming horde
Is a wild call and a free call well away from the diving board;
And all I ask is a quiet day with the bright light shining,
And aerobic mothers dancing near where their kids aren't whining.

I must go down to the gym to swim, on my monthly member's card,
In the fast lane where we pay no heed to the cries of the lifeguard;
And all I ask is a hot tub I can share with a fellow-swimmer,
And a diet lunch and a cat-nap while I keep on growing slimmer.

James Matthew Wilson

from The Fortunes of Poetry in an Age of Unmaking

4. Meter is central to the understanding of the art of poetry in the ancient and medieval and also in the modern views. Rhyme is a graceful complement to meter.

In the ancient period, *memory* appears as a primary element in poetry, whereas, in the modern lyric, *metaphor* comes to the head. But, in both periods, *meter* appears as equally important. Aristotle's comments on poetry as formed of plot more than of meter would become a source for later efforts to cut meter out of the heart of the poetic altogether. Sidney, for example, who defended the beauty of meter so finely, also bluntly denied its essential role for poetry when he spoke of most poets as having "appareled their poetical inventions in that numbrous kind of writing which is called verse." For, he proceeds to parse the word "apparel" to conclude that verse is "an ornament and no cause of poetry." In the context of Aristotle's work, we see this is misguided. In the *Rhetoric*, he tells us that prose should be rhythmical, while poetry is metrical. It is a "cause" indeed.

Meter is a further refinement of the inevitable rhythms of speech. Just as the growing child moves from halting words and phrases to sentences, and the orator formalizes our often ungrammatical speech into balanced periods, so the poet deepens the art of the well-framed sentence of formal speech by subjecting every syllable to measure. Why would the poet do this? Why would it seem so essential an element in poetry, ancient and modern?

The answer is fivefold, and I shall discuss them under the rubrics *memorability, shaping, modality, ordering,* and *deepening.* I shall then offer a brief discussion of the late antique Christian development of rhyme as a distinctive complement to meter in Latin and the European vernacular languages.

As we saw in the second note, meter patterns speech in such

29

a way as to make it *memorable*. It is mnemonic, not just in the metaphysical sense of coming from Mnemosyne, but in the more mundane sense of serving as an aid to memory. It inscribes a formal logic at the core of language so that those literate in meter can often discern what word comes next in a line because it *ought* to come, it fits. But also, the rhythm meter generates is generally resonant and haunting, so that even those unfamiliar with the technical details of prosody can nonetheless benefit from meter's presence. We all know this from our first encounter with nursery rhymes and songs, though we may sometimes mistakenly think it is melody rather than rhythm that causes these things to stick in our head. In the ages of oral, or primarily oral, culture, meter played an essential role in keeping the knowledge of a civilization in being, allowing it to be passed from person to person, generation to generation, through recitation and memorization.

Many will recall Socrates' story of the Egyptian god, Theuth, who has invented writing and promises help men remember things forever. King Thamus replies that it will in fact prove a recipe for forgetting. In the event, they were both correct. Writing would lead to the belated development of prose and the ability to record in lasting fashion ever greater quantities of information. But, it would also result in most persons having a diminished memory and an impoverishment of the arts of memory that sustained culture for millennia. That said, even in the age of Shakespeare, we know that the meter of the dramas continued to play a fundamentally mnemonic role for both the actors and those who attended the plays. This latter group included those who listened, memorized, and then reported what they had heard to publishers, so that pirated editions of the plays could be published.

We shall consider the classical quantitative and modern accentual-syllabic metrical systems in a bit more detail below, but here I would just note the *shaping* role of meter. I have repeatedly distinguished between the formal and material (or content) in these pages. Metrical feet give shape to the metrical line, and metrical lines to the total composition that is a poem. But, it is a strictly *formal* shaping. That is, it brings integrity and order to our words, unity to the poem, without in any way materially delimiting what those words can be or say. A rhetorical strategy like the classical periodic sentence constrains an author to establish certain mathematical proportions and parallel structures at the level of phrase and sentence. However mellifluous may be the result, it directly intervenes in the material content of the speaker. Such is also the case with, most obviously, the parallel structures found in the Psalms and many of the other material strategies free verse poets often embrace in order to give their poems the appearance of integrity (the use of anaphora, for instance). But meter is a purely analytical abstraction from sentence rhythm: "an abstraction from the live flexible movement of spoken language," as James McAuley put it. It establishes a subtle structure of feet that simultaneously gives every syllable a value and the line a perfectly regular order without determining the rhythm as a whole. Relative degrees of stress from syllable to syllable, the use of enjambment across lines, and the regular variations of the grammatical sentence (syntax and length), allow the perfectly regular metrical line to be generative of infinite variety. It is thus the most flexible formal property imaginable, but one which makes the order and integrity of a line of verse unmistakable to the eye and ear.

Another thing meter shapes is our expectations. John Hollander frequently wrote of the "metrical frame" and the modes of poetic form, both of which I comprehend under the rubric, _modality_. By the idea of metrical frame, Hollander intended that the use of certain meters of other poetic forms will create certain expectations in the mind of the reader, because that reader will already associate a particular meter with other, apparently similar, poems he has read, or with a set of familiar conventions. So, for instance, as soon as a reader recognizes a sonnet, the idea of sonnet will form a frame around the individual poem, and this will, in turn, influence its interpretation. We might expect a logical structure built up over three quatrains and concluded with a final, epigrammatic couplet, and we might also expect the subject or "conceit" to be profane or sacred love. Even if those expectations are not met, they will still influence our interpretation of the poem. In the arts, disappointment is a technique.

In speaking of "modes," Hollander refers back to the classical association of particular meters with specific poetic genres. This association was thought to be natural, according to Aristotle, but in our day we see them as more fluid, accumulating within the body of literary conventions, as additional possible sources of meaning. The ballad stanza, for instance, will be associated in most persons' minds with folk song and tale. That Emily Dickinson wrote on themes traditionally part of the lyric mode in this sort of stanza is one source of her work's eerie incongruity between the naïve and the profound.

The three attritutes above are all practical in effect: they help the writer of verse to shape the work, and the auditor or performer to receive and retain it. But the next two attritubtes are of eminently speculative importance regarding the nature of poetry as an art. As we saw, Diotima refers to meter as something specifically given by the muses. What she seems to be referring to is the longstanding perception of the microcosmic order of the line of verse as a good participation in, and revelation of, the *macro-cosmos*, the good *ordering* of being that constitutes the world as a whole. The *musica humana* of the poem is given by the divine music of the muse, and both harmonize with the *music mundana,* the music of the cosmos.

From Pythagoras onward, the Greeks saw the discernment of number in contingent things as an apprehension of truth and being, of the eternal and the unconditioned. To recognize a particular circle — that of a wheel or a pancake for instance — as a circle is to put the mind in immediate contact with the eternal idea of circle that stands free from and above the existence of any actual circular thing. This is an insight found everywhere in Plato and Aristotle, where the perception of this good, true, or (especially) beautiful thing is a portal to the perception of Truth, Goodness, and Beauty writ-large. This Greek insight finds expression in Judaism in the book of Wisdom, where we hear that God "has ordered all things in measure, and number, and weight" (11:21). Divine wisdom is what gives number to the formless void, and our wisdom is the perception of those numbers. In the Christian Platonism of St. Augustine, we see him frequently advert to number as the primary instance in which we see the eternal *Logos* manifest itself in the created world to make that world intelligible to us. He offers a proof of the existence of God through reflection on the intellectual principle of number's presence in material nature. Matter is infinitely divisible, and so cannot be the source of the idea of one, of unity; the idea must come from a transcendent spiritual reality, this is God. When Augustine wishes to understand how the eternal mind of God could produce the flux of historical events, he turns from mathematical numbers to metrical numbers. History unfolds like a line of verse, like a long poem with its metrical feet each distinct from one another (a dactyl, followed by two trochees, and so on, for instance), yet constituting an ordered whole. Just as the poem is one, though its parts rise and fade from existence on the voice, so is the whole span of our life one, though it stretches into the abyss of past and future and seems to exist only in the present moment. Just as the art of poetry is a simultaneous whole in the poet, but a sequential, temporal unfolding in the recited poem, so God is a simple, eternal presence, while his creation is "distended" across time and space.

This classical perception of the "numbers" of verse as indicative of the divine order was so far from being lost on early modern theorists of poetry that, in fact, it seems to have been their principal concern. Campion, even, in his desire to import quantitative meter from Latin to English, was inspired not merely because he found rhyme barbaric, but because he perceived the metaphysical significance of numbers. He tells us, like a good Pythagorean, "The world is made by symmetry and proportion, and is in that respect compared to music, and music to poetry." Sydney speaks of the "well-weighed syllables" of classical quantities, which make of poetry a "planet-like music," that is, a manifestation of the music of the spheres, of the *musica mundana*. Puttenham takes up the theme with enthusiasm. He compares the poet as maker to God, who "made all the world of nought." That they first perceive the order of things and then order it into speech makes them, as we mentioned above, the first in practically every enterprise of civilization:

> Poets therefore are of great antiquity. Then, forasmuch
> as they were the first that intended to the observation of
> nature and her works, and specially of the celestial courses,
> by reason of the continual motion of the heavens, searching
> after the first mover, and from thence by degree coming to

know and consider of the substances separate and abstract, which we will call the divine inelligence or good angels (*daemones*), they were the first that instituted sacrifices of placation, with invocations and worship to them, as to gods, and invented and established all the rest of the observances and ceremonies of religion, and so were the first priests and ministers of the holy mysteries.

He is not done. They lived in chastity and "continual study and contemplation," so that they received divine visions; they were the "first prophets or seers," and all oracles given by the gods came in "metre or verse." Bringing this news of the divine order to the social order, poets also instituted culture and society, as "the first lawmakers of the people and the first politicians," who established commonwealths and brought order, virtue, and peace to the people. In the second book of the *Art*, Puttenham expressly states that proportion (measure or number) is the condition of beauty, and that meter is the proportion of verse. If the poet is the original priest, prophet, and politician — along with so much else — it is only because of meter's "poetical proportion."

This ordering principle, wherein the proportions of meter participate in or manifest by direct analogy the intelligent order of being as a whole, assigns to meter a consummate significance. And yet, it might also seem too simple, as if it were all just a one-to-one correspondence with the heavens. Thus, we should also remark meter's role in the *deepening* of poetry. Every work of art depends for its existence on being beautiful, as Puttenham claims, but beauty is classically understood as *form* and *splendor*. It realizes at once a concrete figure and the intelligible light of universal significance that radiates from it as an irreducible polarity. In contrast to the simple clarity of numbers as such, metrical numbers contribute simultaneously to the specificity and the universal significance of the poem. They particularize and deepen; they bring words to order but they also render them more complex, obscure, and layered with meanings.

John Crowe Ransom spoke of poetry as a rough composite of two parts. Its foundation is the logical or "prose" structure of meaning. But, to this, the poet adds in meter, rhyme, and figurative language, all of which he describes as logically "irrelevant," "local texture." This artificial cramming of what he sometimes calls the "scientific" structue in to the intractable forms of texture ruffles and troubles the poem; it gives to the work those qualities that make it a concrete reality resistant to the rage for abstraction and use. Ransom's account is far too dualistic; as I have insisted, form and content are indeed distinct in reason, but they are one in being. Poets from Virgil to Ben Jonson, to yours truly, may sometimes draft a prose sketch prior to writing the poem itself in meter. But even here that does not mean that the meaning and texture, the content and the form, are distinct, or that the logical structure constitutes the skeleton and the rhyme or meter merely the "texture," the flesh tissue. Many poems begin as a line or two in the mind out of which the larger dimensions of the form emerge. Indeed, many begin as a sound of a metrical rhythm in the ear that only eventually takes on language; such was the origin of Turner's *Genesis*, for instance. The poem is a unified whole; any distinction along these lines is in the reason not the poem, and the sequence of composition has nothing to do with it.

These criticisms noted, Ransom has a point. All things are polysemantic; their meanings are deep, multiple, and at times in tension with one another. Poetry is the paradigmatic art form that exploits this depth found in reality as such in order to reveal and contemplate it. And so, myriad meanings blend within a poem, and meter in particular cross-hatches the "texture" of a poem so that new patterns emerge beyond those of syntax. The poem is a single being where a multitude of signs overlap with one another, and in which distinct orders — some logical some alogical, some in concord, some in tension — coalesce into one.

Rhyme is someting other than meter and is not as obviously essential for poetry. We saw that Campion associated it with the barbarians of the British Isles, who were only with diffficulty civilized by the quantitative orderliness of Latin culture. He associates it also with the "Dark Ages," by which he means the Christian genius of the high Middle Ages. Puttenham and Samuel Daniel also remark the non-classical origins of rhyme, but perceive this as a sign not so much of rudeness as of an inheritance entirely venerable. It is a custom with all the force of common law, but also a new note, writes Daniel, "an excellency added to this work of measure, and a harmony far happier than any proportion antiquity could ever show us." Indeed, it "doth add more grace and hath more of delight than ever bare numbers . . . can possibly yield."

Rhyme first came into use in the Latin of late Christian antiquity, and this seems no coincidence. If the Greeks conceived the world as a Good-Order, and saw poetic rhythm as a participation in it, Christians joined them, but also conceived the world as a grace, a creation, a superabundance produced from nothing and for no other reason than out of God's eternal love. Rhyme itself suggests a superabundance upon meter, an order on top of an order, a grace added to grace. Meter constitutes a necessary order, a grace added to grace. Meter constitutes a necessary order, while rhyme adds a note of gratuity. Like meter, it gives form to lines and stanzas; and, like meter, it cross-hatches a poem with an asyntactical logic; it attains a resonance not only across the lines of a poem, but between poems. In consequence, it adds to the deepening, ordering, modality, and shaping qualities of meter, while also making a poem much more memorable. My youngest son, who is two, is just learning his first poems. How do we proceed? I recite the opening line, and he provides the rhyme word. We shall build from there, no doubt as the first rhymers intended. But, someday, perhaps, he will read Wimsatt's essay, "One Relation of Rhyme to Reason," and conclude that the *mnemonic* function is only the beginning of rhyme's intellectual riches.

5. IN ENGLISH, METER IS TYPICALLY ACCENTUAL-SYLLABIC, IN WHICH METRICAL FEET BRING TO ORDER THE TOTAL NUMBER OF SYLLABLES IN THE LINE AND CREATE A REGULAR PATTERN OF ACCENT OR STRESS.

We discussed, in Chapter 7, the difference between classical quantitative measures, which are always called "meter" in the tradition, and meter such as it is in modern English, which, because usually coupled with rhyme, the tradition often calls the two together either "rhyme" or "rhythm," both of which come from the same root. It should be clear that English meter ("rhyme") and classical quantity ("meter") operate on entirely different principles; one does not derive from the other; and, indeed, they are not even mutually exclusive (Campion's poems in quantitative verse can also be scanned, he made sure, hedging his bet, according to English prosody).

The reader unfamiliar with the working of English versification is referred to the appendix of this book. Here, I wish to make the general note that the main tradition operates according to the principle of accentual-syllabism. Of the Romance languages, French verse has end rhyme but, within the line, attends only to the number of syllables. The classical line of that language, the *Alexandrine,* consists simply of twelve syllables. In English, we attend to syllable count, but also to the number of accents or stresses in a line, and so also to how they are ordered within it. The unit for understanding this combination of syllable and stress counts is the metrical foot. From early on, English prosody has used the ancient Greek names for its feet, but an accentual-syllabic anapest or iamb is something categorically other than the quantitative feet that go by those names.

When Sidney distinguishes this prosody from the numbers of the ancients, he comments that modern verse observes "only number [of syllables], with some regard of the accent, the chief life of it standeth in that like sounding of the words which we call rhyme." Steele notes that "some regard" would be an understatement in reference to English, though it might not be for other modern vernaculars. Anglo-Saxon, much Middle English, and some modern English verse is purely accentual, attending *only* to stress-count. Though the practice varied over time, in brief, unstressed syllables may appear in any number and, sometimes, in any position. Overall, we can say that the earliest prosody in English *would* lead us to think accent was everything, that syllabic-count mattered only in the Romance languages, and that any strict concern with number, length, or weight, would be more appropriate to classical than to modern prosody.

Modern English verse, however, is a product of the slow intermingling of all three traditions. The distinctive development that made this possible as a new system was the introduction of metrical feet, so that both accent and syllable count provide a coordinated principle of order. Note well that the metrical foot is the unified, singular principle; one does not count syllables, then accents, or vice versa. Rather, one counts metrical feet. In consequence, there are many occasions where one might have one or two more or fewer unaccented syllables in a line and yet still have an appropriate number of feet. The syllabic line is sometimes used as an inaudible metrical experiment in our poetry, but, except in those cases where it is coupled with rhyme, it often seems little less arbitrary as a principle or order than does the typographic lineation I discussed in an earlier chapter. The historical development of English poetic rhythm must therfore be understood as the course of a Germanic language with a purely accentual meter coming into contact with the stricter mathematics of classical quantity and Romance language syllabism, so that it finally arrives as a synthesis of the two in the accentual-sylllabic, foot-measured, metrical line. As we shall see, this was no arbitrary event, but one in deep and fruitful concord with the native properties of English. Indeed, Steele, Paul Fussell, and others have argued that it would take a dramatic transformation in the structure of our language to make possible the unseating of accentual-syllabism in favor of some other prosodic system. No such change has yet occurred.

6. ENGLISH ADMITS A VARIETY OF ACCENTUAL AND ACCENTUAL-SYLLABIC METERS, BUT IAMBIC PENTAMETER IS THE MOST PERFECTLY SUITED TO THE NATIVE PROPERTIES OF THE LANGUAGE.

John Hollander once dismissed the efforts of such modern poetic theorists as Yvor Winters to discern a stress pattern in free verse analogous to that of accentual-syllabic meter, observing that,

> to try to scan free verse by counting the number of
> stresses and concluding that, in any event, the poem under
> discussion is roughly assembled of four — or five —
> stressed lines, may be merely to assert a trivial correlation
> built into the structure of English.

It is not uncommon, as we have seen, to hear poets complain of accentual-syllabic meter as if it were some arbitrary imposition upon meter. As I argued in my book on the poetry of Timothy Steele, even defenders of metrical practice, such as Ransom, often give us such a dualistic account of metrical-form as a shaping of otherwise free content, that they too seem to view it as a difficulty, a confinement, a challenge to be embraced, rather than as a principle internal to and in keeping with the nature of the English language. But this is to misunderstand meter and our language alike.

Structural linguistics provides us ample reason to conclude that accentual-syllabic meter is best conceived of as a consciously cultivated efflorescence of properties native to the English language, and that the iambic line is its paradigmatic realization. Casual speech and free verse will, therefore, typically seem like loose examples of it — not because their author was consciously setting about something but because he was speaking English. Steele's guide to prosody, *All the Fun's in How You Say a Thing*, (1999), concisely describes these properties as follows:

> 1) English speech tends "to space stresses at roughly equal intervals"
> 2) The morphology of English words leans toward alternating stress
> 3) The "uninflected" character of our language: word order, rather than word ending, is determinant of meaning. This leads to the intermixing of "particles and pronomials" amid weightier words.

We see these properties at work and lines such as, " I like to play the saxophone, at night"; or, "Whenever Mom gets here, kiss her for me"; or, "The Paparazzi wrecked the conference"; or, "Matthew had chicken Parmesan for lunch." Each of these lines is in iambic contender, though the second has an extra-metrical syllable at the end (a feminine ending) and the third has a trochee in the fourth of its five feet. It is also Steele's contention that this — the iambic pentameter — is the paradigmatic line for English verse, and so let us add a fourth item to our list:

> 4) Iambic pentameter is subtle, flexible, and capacious. It is just long enough for its varieties to be "inexhaustibly exciting," while also perceptible, and irreducible to

shorter parts.

English verse, at its origins, was not only accentual rather than accentual-syllabic, but also typically tetrametric, i.e. four-stressed. As Derek Attridge has observed, even in our day the verse of our popular music is organized according to lines of four stresses. A four-stress line is markedly audible: "Humpty Dumpty sat on a wall," after all, and everyone can thump out the beats of "Jack be nimble, Jack be quick." No one could miss it — even with the two unstressed syllables "on a" scripting the heavy, regular stresses of that first line from *Mother Goose*. In modern verse, our several quatrain (four-line) stanzas tend to group lines of four, and sometimes three, stresses, and in every instance the result will seem to lend itself to song. I still recall some classmate of mine remarking, as if it were a real *coup*, that one could say all of Emily Dickinson to the tune of "Mary Had a Little Lamb." Oh, there is no shortage of melodies to which one could adapt her poems, because they are all in short-lined quatrains, and most of our popular music is built around such lines.

If a four-stress line, accentual or accentual-syllabic, not only conforms to the nature of the language, but seems to provide our verse with its prototype, why would Steele suggest that the iambic pentamter line — with its five feet, or roughly ten syllables and five stresses — is the true paradigm? What earns it the adjectives we reeled off in the fourth point?

At least four attributes come to mind. First, being roughly two syllables longer than the iambic tetrameter, it can accommodate even the longest words in our language. "**Antidis**establishment**ari**an**ism**," our longest word, my parish priest tells me, and though it would make for a very rough line, it would be a pentameter one nonetheless. But, second, being roughly two or four syllables shorter than a hexameter or heptameter line, it will not tend to sound as if it wanted either to break in two even halves or into a tetrameter and a trimeter. If one inserts a pause (a *caesura*), as is very natural to do, at or near the midpoint of these longer lines, one winds up with what will sound like a half a ballad or short-metered quatrain rather than a single long line. The pentameter will therefore be the longest line in our verse that consistently sounds like one line. Every reader will know just where to break these lines so that it appears not as two, but four as Dickinson wrote them:

> Because I could not stop for death, he kindly
> stopped for me
> The Carriage held but just Ourselves and
> Immortality

But who would attempt to chop these verses into smaller units, or extend them to longer?

> She sang beyond the genius of the sea.
> The water never formed to mind or voice,
> Like a body wholly body, fluttering
> Its sleeves; and yet its mimic motion
> Made constant cry, caused constantly a cry,
> That was not ours although we understood,
> Inhuman, of the veritable ocean.

We hear pauses, but, for a reason we shall consider, they are highly irregular ones and float free of the line-unit.

This leads us to our third, and most important, point. Though the iambic pentameter normally consists of an even number of syllables, each iamb comprises one unstressed, followed by one stressed, syllable, for a total of five metrical feet. This odd number tends to keep the line from feeling rigidly symmetrical, and therefore prevents it from seeming to break up into two audible units that might as well be separate lines. It also encourages a variability of syntax as words and phrases of different length run across the regular pattern of metrical feet in the line, and across lines, through the use of enjambment. In consequence, while the iambic pentamter may be the longest line we can normally hear as a line, it is also a line that can be rendered especially subtle, almost inaudible *as a line*, if the flow of enjamed iambs is drawn out long enough. The difference between the early and mature Shakespearean iambic pentameter is that between one in which each line stands out as a rigid whole and another in which the metrical line quietly gives minute order to the long cadences and complex sentence of extended periods. The blank verse of Milton raised this practice to a principle, where "the sense [is] variously drawn out from one verse into another." Overall, what one discovers in studying the use of the iambic pentameter line (as the poet Robert Shaw shows in his history of the line, *Blank Verse* (2007)), is an astonishing versatility from Marlowe to Wordsworth and Wallace Stevens, where the meter can become as assertive or subtle, as musical or prosaic, as the occasion demands.

A fourth quality presents itself. Granted, we say, the three mentioned attributes of the English language make an alternation of stressed and unstressed syllables inevitable in our speech. But, according to the third attribute, it would seem as if small, unstressed monosyllabic words would cluster around rarer, stressed syllables, in semantically weightier words. The regular alternation of unstressed and stressed syllables, in the iamb, would not seem to be our only option. First of all, meter could be trochaic, alternating stressed-unstressed, and, second, it could run with more than one unstressed syllable before each accented one — what is called anapestic meter. Trochaic and anapestic meters are, in fact, the only plausible alternatives to the iambic line, in English. They just lack the versatility of the iamb, and especially that of the iambic-pentameter. Why?

In any effort to write the trochaic line, we will quickly find that most sentences start with an unstressed syllable, that relatively few words end on a falling or feminine rhythm ("rhythm" is one such word), and, on those occasions when a sentence does start with a stress, it is easy, even routine, to follow with two unstressed syllables. If all three of these conditions obtain, one will find it more natural to write an iambic line with a trochee inserted in the first foot (an inverted first foot, as it is called in the appendix) than to attempt a completely trochaic measure. When a trochaic meter is used, one will find oneself stressing, at the beginning of the line, words that would otherwise feel, in the context of syntax, light or unstressed. "If I die before I wake" is trochaic tetrameter, but to hear it thus you must say, "IF," and the line still ends with the stress, as if it wanted to return to the iambic norm. This can be used to great effect. We have no shortage of trochaic poetry in English. But, it is simply not as versatile as the iambic norm.

The more interesting case is the anapestic line. While none of us speaks in all iambs or all anapests in our every day chatter, it would seem that our speech *does* fall closer to a sequence of iambs with occasional anapests than to the opposite. When language is measured in iambs, it tends to sound more finally wrought, formal, and impressive:

> When to the sessions of sweet silent thought
> I summon up remembrance of things past,

When we order words into anapests, we find two things. First, it is almost impossible to use only anapests. Iambs keep slipping in here and there. Second, the result sounds more like a horse galloping than it does the speech of the classically educated army colonel riding on her back. Of course, sometimes a gallop is just what one wants, as in the stanzas from a classic poem by X. J. Kennedy:

> In a prominent bar in Secaucus one day
> Rose a lady in skunk with a topheavy sway,
> Raised a knobby red finger — all turned from their
>   beer —
> While eyes bright as snowcrust she sang high and
>   clear:
>
> 'Now who of you'd think from an eyeload of me
> That I once was a lady as proud as can be?
> Oh I'd never sit down by a tumbledown drunk
> If it wasn't, my dears, for the high cost of junk.'

We all want to visit such a bar from time to time; we just would not want our poetry to abide there forever.

7. METER, OR VERSE, IS THE CONSTITUTIVE FORMAL ELEMENT OF POETRY AND ALSO THE MEANS OF ITS PERFECTION, BUT POETRY IS A WHOLE TRANSCENDENT OF ANY ONE OF ITS PARTS.

A poem is a composite being, made from parts that the reason can distinguish even within the whole. But it is also a true unity, a whole greater than the sum of its parts. As I mentioned in the third chapter, the modernists had thought this entailed an absolute identity of form and content, and their attempts to realize it were intended to be a distinguishing aspect of the work, a mark of its achieved consciousness. Winters, who was often considered a reactionary in his day and who certainly rejected many developments of the modernist period, nonetheless draws on the poetic theory of the proto-modernist Stéphane Mallarmé to express the character of the poem as a fusion, a simple unity. He tells us,

> The poem, to be perfect, should . . . be a new word . . . a
> word of which the line . . . is merely a syllable. such a word
> is, of course, composed of much more than the sum of
> its words (as one normally uses the term) and its syntax. It
> is composed of an almost fluid complex . . . a
> relationship involving rational content, cadences, rhymes,
> juxtapositions, literary and other connotations, inversions,
> and so on, almost indefinitely. They partake of the fluidity
> and unpredictability of experience and so provide a means
> of treating experience with precision and freedom.

An absolute unity: a single new word. But also, a composite whole: a "fluid complex." Whose parts can nonetheless be distinguished: "a relationship."

If the modernists experimented with new ways of making that would realize that unity, they need not have done so. Those cultures informed by the Christian Platonist tradition have always granted to the being of the poem, to aesthetic form in general, an irreducible integrity, even as they have also accepted the rational distinctions between form and matter. This is why, as Remi Brague tells us in his *Eccentric Culture* (2002), the Romans did not just preserve the ideas of their Greek forbearers, but their complete works, keeping them whole and commenting on them in part, rather than "digesting" them, and retaining only the parts they found useful. So also is it why the medieval Christians preserved the works of pagan antiquity whole, or tried to. They did not wish merely to harvest parcels of information they found true but to hold onto works in their full aesthetic integrity, and for the sake of their inexhaustible depths. Our tradition has always assumed that things, including works of art, insofar as they are beings, are also indivisibly one. It has always retained this aspect of metaphysical realism, despite the atomizing and materializing tendencies so ubiquitous in modern Western culture.

It is for this reason that we finally had to dissent from the otherwise attractive essentialism of Cunningham, discussed in chapter 7. Cunningham wished to identify some basic element, some minimal definition, that would unmistakably identify poem as a poem, and the result was the phrase "composition and meter." Poetry may do all kinds of things beyond meter, and these things will make a particular tone more or less good, but, though all of this is part of the tradition built upon the essential bedrock of "composition in meter," it is not to be taken as part of that essence. But this is inadequate. What makes a poem a poem is the actualized unity of the various elements that come together to make a composite whole. It would be strange to say that some of those elements belong to the essence while others do not. It would be, as we said, to attend to material causes but to reject final causality as a way of knowing; but all real knowledge is bound up with the principal of finality. We cannot know what poetry is only by turning to its beginnings; we see things through to their end.

So, then, how shall we define poetry? It is abundantly clear from the previous five chapters that most contemporary poets have failed to grasp its essence, and what they have produced in consequence is, on the whole, an embarrassment. Their work discredits the historical dignity assigned to poetry as does it make poetry seem an elusive, indeed an insubstantial, thing.

We have offered six notes toward a definition. It is the purpose of this seventh to clarify how they all not only fit together, but hold together as a transcendent whole. Let us say, then, that meter is the primary formal element of poetry. History is the basis of reflection in the Aristotelian tradition, and our history shows us that meter is what originally constitutes this thing called poetry. It comes first in time, if nothing else.

Aristotle himself, we saw, tells us that meter is not sufficient to constitute the essence of poetry — you could versify Herodotus and still have history — but I am not sure he's right. Those who read Lucretius's *On the Nature of Things,* read it first and foremost as a poem, and secondarily as a work of Roman epicurean philosophy; even those who do read it primarily *for* its philosophy still read it *as* a poem. If someone did set the stories from the *Histories* down in verse, it would be greeted as a poem, and probably a very good one. Furthermore, any reader of Herodotus will see that, in his representation of Solon, the historian is instructing us that the study of history is itself a means to rise from "singulars" to "universals," just as all thinking in the Aristotelian philosophical tradition presumes to do. Solon has traveled the world and learned the life stories of many men; therefore, we are told, he has the wisdom to find happiness and pronounce which men have best attained it (King Croesus has not). So, while I agree with Aristotle that poetry is indeed "philosophical," I think he errs in thinking meter insufficient to make a work a poem as does he err in thinking the historian, in principle, lacks a philosophical dimension, however much most historians may seem to.

One philosophical, if not historical, reason meter comes first and poetry is that it is, as Diotima tells us, "the part the Muses give us." As we have seen, if meter is in one sense a further refinement of language, it is also a manifestation of the primordial intelligible order of the *cosmos.* In consequence, it is *shaping,* in other words, it holds the poem together making it an ordered whole, a *microcosm.* And it is also *ordering* and *deepening,* giving to the poem a kind of final perfection, a splendor of and beyond the form that is constitutive of its existence and beauty. It opens onto the *macrocosm* at every pulse. I have argued elsewhere that beauty, in our experience and in reality, comes first and also last. My argument here is that we may say just that about meter. It comes first, from the depths of history, to order speech into poetry, but it is also the final perfection of the poem, a gift from an order beyond us, giving it a resonance with its origins in the true, good, and beautiful order of reality as a whole.

If meter comes first and last, it may be said to envelop all the other possible elements of the poetic essence: its memorability, its capacity for storytelling, for the representation of interior states, and for imitation (of human action or experience, *mimesis*), and metaphor (trope). None of these things would have come to be identified with poetry, had poetry not first been constituted by meter. But, it was, and they have. They are indeed elements that help poetic meter to attain its final cause, the perfection of the poem as a complete being. They do not stand outside the essence of the poem as poem, but help it to become more fully itself. The meter may provide a basis for them, but they also provide a basis for the meter. When we encounter any of these individual elements, they will appear to us as more or less poetic.

Let us phrase it this way. Meter constitutes the paradigm of poetry, as the muse-given art of poetry constitutes the paradigm of making. Just as non-poetic acts of making participate in the paradigm of poetry by degrees of analogy, so will non-metrical compositions potentially appear as poems to us, despite the absence of that paradigmatic element. Winters referred to *Moby-Dick* as an epic, and others have referred to other novels and films in the same terms. And emotional speech is sometimes praised as "the song of one's heart." A work in free verse — lineated like Charles Wright's work, or in straight prose like some of Baudelaire's compositions — will appear to us as a poem because of its cadences and schemes, its use of tropes, or of moods and modes proper to the conventions of the lyric. We might be tempted, strictly speaking, to say these things are poems only by analogy, but in fact we will all experience them as poems, even if we soon become conscious of something vital missing. They will appear to us as poems *on the whole,* despite the absence of such a foundational and perfected element as meter. This has been a book about poetry, after all, and those radical limit cases I discussed I did as instances of degraded, vacuous, and pretentious poetry. I could only have been speaking analogically.

What is poetry in its fullness, then? Approaching it from the outside, we see that it is a hypostatic union of the made and the given, the gift passively received and the art actively undertaken, the human craft and the divine origin. This alone suffices to explain why poem is always more than itself, a duality in unity, a perfectly intelligible mystery. Looked at from within, at its heart, we see that this union of art and gift result in something that has the character of the trinity. Memory, meter, and metaphor live together in a kind of circumincession. Meter is already the first instance of memory, gathering and holding parts together as a whole. It it is already the first metaphor, signifying what is beyond itself by its numbered nature. And so, memory and metaphor are at once other than meter and continuous with it. Meter may be present at the beginning, but, as first and last, it holds all together.

But this interior heart of poetry is always going out beyond itself. The three attributes enable poetry to reach out to, by their own and absolute natures, the most far flung and contingent of things — the remembered or imagined plots of story, the curious analogies of trope, the peculiar specificities of English or any language that give to their respective meters a strange necessity. Therefore, while, in one sense, it is beyond the tripartite essence of poetry, they are also, in another sense, proper to it that poetry can tell stories or represent interior states, can imitate and reveal, inquire and persuade, please and instruct — and do many other things besides. In each case, we have a potency, a possible function, diffused from the interior nature of poetry, that will lead a poem — the particular, individual poem — to become more fully itself.

The notes toward a definition of poetry I have offered here stake some big claims. Poems can tell us the stories we need to know, can help us remember them, and can put us in contact with the highest truths of reality. They can manifest those truths in meter and represent them by the power of metaphor. Poetry is a mode of contemplation and inquiry, what is normally called *dialectic*, even as it is also the furthest refinement of grammar and *rhetoric*. Its meter and rhyme are a natural ordering of language, and in conformity with the native properties of our tongue, but it is also a grace that transcends these things and reminds us of another Word. It is a craft of many parts, but also a real unity, a whole that is more than the sum of its parts.

All this we have seen traduced in our day, by the contemporary academy and by contemporary poets. I hope this book will seem a worthy response to their assaults, and that it will summon those with a love of well-made things, with a hunger for beauty and an interest in truth, not to wash their hands of a great art form just because its present predicament is so appalling. Were there no more good poems to be written, the art of poetry would command our attention simply because of those we already have. But good poems *are* being written. Richard Wilbur's "Blackberries for Amelia" and "For C."; Mary Jo Salter's "Welcome to Hiroshima" and "Goodbye, Train"; Helen Pinkerton's "On Taddeo di Bartolo's 'Triptych of the Madonna and Child'"; Timothy Steele's "The Color Wheel" and "A Muse"; Ned Balbo's "Peacock"; Dana Gioia's "Haunted" and "The Angel with the Broken Wing"; these are just ten poems from recent decades that deserve the reader's attention now and to live in the memory henceforth. In an age that considers pure possibility the only true freedom, and the unmaking of every achievement an act of liberation, I cannot speculate what will be the fortune of poems such as these, much less the future fortunes of poetry as an art. That has not been my task. I have rather sought to explain what has gone wrong, to show us what we have had and what we have rejected, and to advocate its restoration. The rest is not up to me.

Ashley Anna McHugh

The Archeology of Grief

Kfer HaHoresh (8500 – 6750 B.C.)

Dust clouds the air around the site,
clean rasp of trowels.
                    Nothing can hide.

Reveal the mother, curled around
her infant's ribcage — cradled with care.
No skulls on the bodies buried here.

But just below, in the hallowed ground,
uncover the unborn bones, still there,
as slight as feathers — and then despair

as the sunset hoods its stunning glare,
dust clouding the site, choking the air.
This is our past. We cannot hide.

CHAD ABUSHANAB

Girl Found Dead in the Sequatchie Valley

"The victim's parents declined to comment."
— The Middle Tennessee Courier

They found her body lying here
   between the skeletons of pine.
      As though by some design
  she died in Fall, the time of year

when shadows kissed her thin, pale wrists,
   and the sun, at last, turned cold and white
      like filled with frozen light.
  The talk is vague, but most insist

her boyfriend led her to the hollow
   at night, they had a fight, that she
      was newly pregnant, and he
  was mad, and madness is what followed.

But the stories only flirt with reason,
   and the local papers let it go,
      leaving these woods to know
  and to forget. Now's the season

when the dead wind shakes the leafless trees,
   the purple clover turns to brown,
      and all the lights in town
  look far away, like listless eyes.

And I wonder what's out here to learn
   besides the silence of these hills
      once final sunlight fills
  the valley like a broken urn?

It cannot hold. The light escapes
   as though it's liquid through a sieve,
      and I want to believe —
  as all gets tangled in the drapes

of night — in wholeness, if not peace.
   The girl is dead. Her voice is lost
      in all the stories tossed
  like leaves when autumn strips the trees.

What happened here, I'll never know.
   The valley holds such secrets dear.
      Her love, her screams, her fear
  and blood all make the kudzu grow.

Moira Egan

Tabu

I wasn't quite a badass yet (in fact
report cards came in, almost always A's;
Behavior: Excellent), and yet a crack
(subliminal) was slinking its slow way
toward taking down the perfect girl façade.

Narcissus never had a chance, the mirror
funhoused, not a friend. The books I read
spread-eagled in the fields, wild rose and clover,
would do me, do me in, Totems, Taboos
and Discontents, and Fear of Flying, dusk
transition, homework done, to how I'd use
my body, gleaming, civet, amber, musk.

I ran off to New York, the streets alone,
exotic breezes, neroli and clove.
We woke the morning after, shared an orange.
He wondered why I'd cried. He hadn't known.

Sofia M. Starnes

The New World

At first, our resurrection brewed
beside a lamplight at our door,
then came a pivoting, a need

to send out parties to the moon,
wide open in her swollen hours.
There, in her small suburban shore —

a frozen track, a bleached white flag —
we laid the blueprint of our town,
thin louvered blinds and frontal

stones; there we arranged our green-
house domes (among new mannequins
and stores), tulips in ornamental

glass, to gaze at from our windows.
But that was then (we've wandered past)
outlying has become outlast,

the loss of glossy enterprise
in an abandoned plaza. Once more,
the sails, the sweetheart ships; once

more, our skillets wrapped in silk,
our bluest sandals pushed to rest
in a distant carbon village. The earth,

white porch or blest tempestuous
town, must blow her final farewell kiss . . .
She will not fret too much, I think,

how far we go, how burnt our reach;
for near the edges of her streams,
her caves are set for evening fires:

there sleep her children (leaf on leaf),
their fathers watch, and wait, and keep.

Dolores Stewart

Directions

You'll need some stones to sew inside your hems
or else you cannot drown. Those billowing skirts
will keep you waltzing on a wave of dreams
when what you want to do is sink in hurt.
Smooth, heavy, inert masses. Anger. Losses.
How many does it take? Depression. Fears.
Enough to trip you where the traffic crosses
or crash your loveboat on a fogbound shore.
Collect them all your life. Let not one go
uncounted. Heavy failures. Jealous longings.
When dawn arises with its fist of rose,
hang on, for pity's sake, to weights and wrongs.
Otherwise you'll be too light, too airy, too spry,
too easy in your skin and apt to fly.

KATHRYN JACOBS

Salt Memories

A Pickled City, salted and preserved.
Which means the War on Snow commences. Rows
of blue-chip pebbles melting into streaks
leave sun-dried salt-flats, while a man-made sea

runs gutter-ward in ornate, patterned swerves
as sleepy drivers err. And salt-melt flows
into the landscaped triangles, grass meek
beneath the onslaught, sinking crunchily

like frozen sponges. Life is hard on grass
no matter what (and on the rest of us),
but when you live on islands — go on, taste;
nobody's looking. Nothing can erase
tongue-recollections; a tear-sodden face
has just that tang. I miss you. What a waste.

JAMES HAINES

Muse

She likes the long maple workbench, the tools
and stickered boards. She likes to watch a flitch
re-sawn, opened, and matched up with its mate
to read as if a book. She likes the rules, squares,
and marking knives, the sliding bevel gauge,
the trammel points and templates of French curves,
the lines they make for chisels, shaves, and saws.
She likes the hand-stitched rasp, the way its teeth
perfect a shape; the linseed oil and turpentine,
coat after coat, and how the pumice rubs
a luster that invites an eye to look,
a hand to linger. She likes the finished piece
placed in its place, to have it seen, as if
to speak of what it means to be complete.

THOM SATTERLEE

Green Lights

She made the light at Lewiston, the one
at River, too, saw green at Lyon Street
and would have turned for home had she not begun
to see this drive down Main as incomplete
until she knew how many lights she'd make
just driving at this slow, mid-morning pace
through town, light traffic, nothing more at stake
than the look of scorn she'd find on her husband's face
for taking longer than she'd promised to,
and so she crossed over Oak before it changed,
then Dellinger, then Ellicott, on through
Court, Jackson, Liberty — the lights arranged
themselves for her at Swan, then Harvester —
green, all green, from one end of town to the other!

N.S. THOMPSON

Mr Larkin on Photography

But o, photography! as no art is,
Faithful and disappointing!

I like high windows and my *Penthouse* (sweet
Illusions where I'm never overlooked)
And if my darling ever wandered in
She knows that this could never be a sin,
A simple gander, not my goose well cooked,
Unless . . . *But look at that one, what a treat!*

(But most of this goes on inside my head
And even if I fiddle with my zip
And think of some mid-afternoon relief,
My cover is a cotton handkerchief.)
While ogling them I let the pages flip
To see the girls bounce into life not dead-

Pan static parodies of men's desire.
And should I like to see them less well dressed
Or coupling like a chimpanzee or hog?
I see myself a different kind of dog,
A seedy bachelor, perhaps, at best,
Not brute with any brute that they could hire;

One that prefers his women less exposed,
Still clinging to some decorousness, face
Alluring, well made-up, a breast or rump
To tease me for the mental grind and bump,
Excited by what lies behind the lace.
I know, of course, that everything is posed:

Both sides gleam with a smile of satisfaction:
They in the gentle art of feigning it,
Me in the solitary act of pleasure
Knowing well this will never be the measure
Of what the world is pleased to call my wit.
And so my mind is coupled with the action

Until it finds it's pleasantly relieved,
Controlling all the movements with an eye
To seeing eyelids flutter as I smile,
Remaining clear-eyed by a country mile
And knowing what it leaves me, which is my
Imagination and the less deceived.

STEPHEN SCAER

Fence Building

Though we've been next-door neighbors quite a while,
your shoulders hunch each time I say hello,
and I don't think I've ever seen you smile
or heard you laugh. Whenever we have snow
you wait until I've shoveled out my drive
to blow yours in. I see you every night
scowling at me through my panes, so I've
decided to remove you from my sight
before I'm tempted to reciprocate.
I'll put up with your Charles Manson stare
long enough to quarantine your hate
by nailing shut the only view we share.
In you I recognize too much of me —
a funhouse image I don't want to see.

STEPHEN BLUESTONE

Mad to be Saved

Christopher Smart to Jack Kerouac

The road's rough, Jack, yet we keep on;
we burn and testify; we yawp non-stop;
we stay the course; we ride, no matter what,
two spirits in irons and lashed of the Lord;
our winding paths, I know, will reach the shore,
the restful end, the promised all-is-well.
Listen: *bell well toll soul lawn moon boon* . . .
You and I, good friend, are nightingales;
I swear it, Jack, we rhyme in syllables,
in consonants and vowels, of tongues beyond.
I stopped the other day with Mr. Pope
— a true poet, a blossom in God's eye —
and watched the flowers on a trellis turn.
Those Twickenham roses knew their gardener.

PETER COOLEY

Nostalgia Piece

Give me another morning when I'm ten,
when the world comes to me as apple trees.
First day of summer and ambition
tells me to climb the dozen in my yard
before supper. And now I'm scaling space,
the first branch, then the higher, each tree higher.

All that summer in my remembering
the apple trees are lifting their white blossoming
without my asking, without my ever asking!

This is before my body and its world
takes me by surprise, before the girls,
before insatiables, when there's no time before.

First day of summer. Blue wind and blue wind.

Before the perishings in everything.

QUINCY R. LEHR

End Times

You never asked to walk upon the water,
never claimed it, never went to church,
while those with messianic claims made do
with family yachts, the way it's always done.

No one slouched to Bethlehem. No beast
was born. It was concocted in a lab
and molded into shape by focus groups
who like their evil slightly more dressed-down.

From prototype to archetype, the myth
went through its iterations. First a chant,
it turned into a liturgy, then changed
into a biker rally aimed at teens.

No Armageddon — quite; more a collage
of video footage spread across the globe,
interspersed with ads, responsible
demands for extra troops to "get things done."

When we noticed, it was like a tax
due a few months off; unopened bills;
a forecast of a heat wave; promises
of moderation from the offices

that thought up this — either euphemistic
or to the tune of Baby Boomer rock,
with claims of greatness, demands for increments,
even though we haven't got much time.

ALLISON ADAIR

He Waited for Days

When he was five or maybe six, their car
broke down in Pennsylvania. They rolled
to rest beside a silo. Served her right
for dreaming somewhere else, somewhere new —
there's rotting corn spilled out in every road.
But this was still the forties, and his mother
told him to hide — no porch light, no one called
out. Leaving was decisive — fathers did it.
He watched his mother's dark familiar shape
grow dim, then unfamiliar, not a body more
a wind that uproots fields and just moves on.
She pitched the keys skyward to buy time,
by morning, when he found them, she'd be lost.
He was alone then, five or six, or less.

ALLISON ADAIR

Lymphoma

I
An oyster's pearl marks not one crime, but two:
loose mollusk-beard, slow-sweeping the sea floor,
unclenches, first, to risk its jelly drag.

The body's weak, pink water-song. Angles grift
in, sudden friction in the private mouth —
but don't we know that scuff? How, to protect

itself, sore flesh enfolds its own intruder
tenderly? Grit fricative against
raw red swell. It's a hard swaddling

for everyone — kaleidoscopic oil
transforming all that rough rasp into shell.

Appointments come and go. Cameras probe.

Despite low tide, barnacle valves sway
easy, as if the moon were here to stay.

II
On the day I visit the surgeon I dress
my daughter in her most precocious clothes.
We talk about my throat as if it's chance
not who you know, or who that person knows.

But I think I'll convince him to save me
with a toddler's capelet. It hurts to laugh
by now. Last night she asked _what's slavery?_

then played "triage." Her doll stifled a cough.
A young girl needs her mother. Even if
I don't know what to say, how to answer.
Who else can show how a body stiffens
into a question mark? Just tell her: cancer.

Tell her the source and end to wonder lie
in her hands. That, I, too, asked — no, screamed it — *why*

DAN CAMPION

Tomato Vines

We cage them now. They used to be staked out,
tied up with old dishrag or T-shirt strip
to lumber scrap, as soon as first green sprout
and flower showed which way the fruit would tip.
The stem, as prickly as a boar's-hair brush,
might scrape the fingers that would tie the knot,
and certainly perfumed them with a lush
bouquet of mint and grass and compost rot.
The clusters hidden in among the leaves,
when brought to light, might wear a strangled look,
garrotted by the knotted rag that weaves
from packet seeds to garden plot to cook.
We'd pick the red, ripe fruit and leave the rest,
and loose or cinch the knot as we thought best.

SIMON HUNT

Sam and Andre

Samuel Beckett and Andre "the Giant" Roussimoff,
near Grenoble, circa 1958

At twelve, the little giant was
the butt of such sharp ridicule
he cried while waiting for the bus
that brought farm kids to town for school.
At six-foot-three and eighteen stone,
the child could barely fold his frame
into the seats, and he was known
by everything except his name.
Most days, a neighbor stopped his truck
and gave the lad a ride — a slim,
dour Irishman who'd had great luck
in writing for the stage. To him,
the boy was just the awkward son
of his paid laborer, a man
he owed some money to — and one
does kindnesses the way one can . . .

I've made up half of this, you know.
The rest's what Andre said once to
some journo who had caught the show
and stayed to grab an interview.
By then, of course, the giant had
become a star through throwing men
of normal size. Life wasn't bad —
although his bones all ached — and when
the movies needed, say, a troll
or ogre, now and then they'd call.
But bulk and vodka took their toll,
and he died young.

Now, after all
these years, the story's only traces
are on the internet and where
costars, once dubbed tomorrow's faces,
nostalgically, with graying hair,
reflect within a DVD's
new "Legacy Edition" band,
narrating offscreen memories
they heard, at best, at second hand.
One such considered Andre quite
the raconteur, a real E-ticket,
who told him late one sozzled night
the playwright only talked of cricket.

Why not? It's tempting now to say
the writer and the freak-child spoke
of isolation, painful day,
the seasons' funny, awful joke:
the tree has leaves and then does not.
But both our characters are dead.
This little tale is all we've got:
This figment from a giant's head?
This laureate who never said.

JEFF HOLT

A Madwoman

Some of you here imagine drama, even
envy us in ignorance of how
true madness feels. It doesn't rise with seven
burning wheels and set our brains aglow.

Rather, it withers deep within us like
a dying lily. Though we weep, it still
refuses water. Shriveled, scared, alike,
we simply sit and stare, wait for the pills

that might rouse us, might make us functional.
This takes some burden from our families.
How do we feel? How does a knife, gone dull,
feel to your touch? We wade through miseries

we can no longer name. But say we're well.
We've been to church. We know the flames of Hell.

ROB JACKSON

You Outweigh Me

now, with steroids' cravings
and no constraints on sweets and beers.
Your scale tops off at seventy-nine
kilograms and years.

And why not? There's no holding back.
From cordial six to size sixteen
you've filled your plate and friends so full
each day is Halloween.

I called your cell from baggage claim.
Though parked you let it keep on ringing.
A son would understand that Cheetos
need finishing.

The walnuts rest like tiny brains
in pieces buried in your purse.
Your Reader's Digest says their flesh
stops Alzheimer's and worse.

With all the deviled eggs devoured
you dig out turkey bones to strip.
Each sandwich leaves you searching for
some Miracle Whip.

In truth it's only you who's coping
with gain and loss and pending heartache.
You're celebrating each last supper
through Death by Chocolate Cake.

You face with Epicurean peace
malignant growth inside your head.
With grace and taste you choose to pass
your final course by breaking bread.

BILL GLOSE

On Patrol

Just imagine you're on a nature walk
as you set out in dark across the sand,
body-armored, weapon cupped in hand,
each man in the wedge forbidden to talk
except to yell a warning if something
goes amiss. Otherwise, the goggled green
reminds you of the forest from your dreams,
free of thorns that bite, thistles that sting.
Easy to pretend you're scanning a copse
filled with nestling birds whose love songs linger
even as SAFE slips to SEMI, and finger
slips to trigger, eyes scanning the rooftops
for heat blooms of robed men who wish you dead
but are willing to give their lives instead.

BILLY REYNOLDS

Psalm: & they shall smoke

His dying breaths consume me as that outer
dark once did, stung water beads down the
windshield, guardrails & verticals drops
slashed by headlights, his cigarette lit &
lifted toward that hair of night air that
made its home-late whistle. His smoke

was love at my eyes, one more hard pull &
last flick in the ashtray. I would miss it,
the sting in my eyes, the fragrant windy night.
I had to look back, the way it flew out &
betrayed the oiled road scarred & cracked,
the way it gave, briefly, firecracker light.

I know words as smoke and fire, stick &
flashlight, cool wind in a dry season,
rain & wet & water, rain hammering
the water. I know I can't stop yammering,
all morning & into the afternoon.
If I keep going, he will not die.

I helicopter to his lawless breath,
a sentry at the host his body made of breath
& breath of that room. I know my ear
near his shaved chest modeled in scar tissue
when they had cut him & pulled out the heart.
I know he could have died then years ago.

I hold his chapped fish lips in steady regard,
those seconds I wait for the next breath
held back in the stalled traffic of his lungs.

I dwell there in each breath's take and due.
I tarry in that one-note, worn out music
I will lie down once and play by heart.

HORACE

Ode I.11

Leucon, no one can ever know his fate —
not you, not me. So don't open the gate
that makes a man read tea leaves or sing hymns.
This could be our last winter — then again,
we might live decades and see many more
pound the white sand here on this Tuscan shore.
So do what you must do. Trim back your vines
and don't invest in hope. The sands of time
run even as we speak! We only share
this day. The future is no one's affair.

Translated by David Landrum

JOHN RIDLAND

Another Art

The art of finding is a hard one, mister,
harder by half than learning how to lose.
Try finding your lost uncle or dead sister.

And "finders keepers" has a catch: resist or
your world fills up, you won't know which is whose,
or where is what? You'll never find it, mister.

You found a sweetheart once; of course you kissed her,
but when you pressed and said she had to choose,
she split, because she "loved you like a sister,"

not for the way you came on like a twister
crunching a farmhouse. Now you're sunk in ooze,
try finding your way back to Kansas, mister!

The fact they've raised on both your heels a blister
means that you won't leave Oz in those red shoes.
Too large to lance, each one might be a cyst or

tumor. The yellow brick road's only glister.
No lie: you've learned to sing the Blistered Blues.
The art of finding is a hard one, mister,
but now you've mastered it — meet your dead sister.

JOHN RIDLAND

Agamemnon's Return

Like a little tin god from Olympus you turn up,
The King who killed your daughter to kick-start the winds
That blew the expedition across the water
To Troy. Kissed on the cheek by a silver-headed

Woman, the Queen, your old bald dome reweaves
The plural, many-epitheted seas,
Returns, accustomed to this quick, alert
Look-about, wary even in homecoming.

The woman's hair is as smooth as brushed aluminum.
Who is she now? Who are you? Yourself, old nose-cone,
Washed in the deep bleaches of sea-foam,
Sitting down amid the clatter of domestic crockery?

There is no mistaking that rumble under the tea-cups
Set on the black-lacquered tray, a souvenir.
The sugar cubes are dissolving like granite blocks,
Crumbling backwards into the raw cane syrup,

Which laps against the enameled cliffs of your teeth
In this unexpectedly red Mediterranean.
The exact sense of the frieze is about to be known.
She was no Penelope; you are not Odysseus.

The god takes off, leaving you only human.
Come: you have voyaged unimagined distances.
Relax: step down into this scented bath,
The handmaidens waiting with towels and knives.

STEPHEN PALOS

Sleeping Bear

We saw it on the dunes: it was no dream:
a brown bear, climbing, clawing at the sand,
advancing all its weight with all its muscle,
and losing ground each step, and hardly moving
after all, and never turning back.

We watched the brute go on like this an hour,
the growing shadows, sea spray in the air,
never certain — was it chasing something?
The dune — it was a dune and nothing more.
A few stiff plants and sand on sand on sand . . . .

Only now, years later, do I see
in my memory, just what it sought:
once, turning back to it, I saw it climbing,
clawing at the sand — how small it seemed —
and dull stars waiting over the horizon.

HERB WAHLSTEEN

Chiaroscuro

The city seems asleep. He kisses Eve
and says that they should take a drive up to
the foothills. Adam often dreams of days
and ways that were. He grew up with thick woods
all round yet moved five years ago to this
too populated and polluted city.
While standing up, they turn toward the window.
The moon's light drenches the apartment roofs
surrounding their block-long apartment house.
"Tonight, the foothills must be sparkling like
large, dark jewels," Eve smiles, "Yes, I'm in the mood
for taking an aesthetic, country walk
beneath the moon."

                It's a warm, winter night
in Southern California. Adam closes
the drapes and gets his keys. He locks their door,
and they're soon riding on the freeway. Eve
begins a conversation by saying,
"There aren't too many people now-a-days
who think like us, Adam." She pauses, then
says, "It's too bad that on this bright, warm night
most people are at home in front of screens."
Adam replies with, "Many people are
afraid to step outside their door. The ones
who aren't go to some crowded, public place.
I'm glad you like when we walk through the foothills.
The air's still chaste, and the quiet there really
relaxes me. I love the interplay
of light and shade up in that great space. With the
moon bright like this, it's magical. Emotions

seem conjured by Pan's unpredictable spells.
The only thoughts that trouble me are thoughts
of meeting an insane snake or human.
Old nature and old fate are always factors
that are disturbingly inconstant. They
can bless or they can kill. Well, I hope we'll
enjoy an Epicurean evening."

Soon, they're both silent like the ride. They leave
the freeway, rolling up Old Country Road.
They drive up it until its dead end. They
then park their car on the deserted street.
Before them, east, is a wide, weedy plain.
To the near right are fine, suburban homes.
Near left are aromatic orange groves.
In the far southeast is a gully with
a fair-sized creek and eucalyptus trees.
To the northeast is where they want to walk.
There wanders a dirt road beneath homes that
resemble palaces. Unlike those small,
one-story houses in the flats, these standing
here soar three stories high. They have bay windows
and pseudo-spires. They're all built too closely
together in the typical way that
it's done in Southern California. The
dirt road inclines by slow degrees. Suddenly,
a galaxy of city lights ascends
into the startled viewer's vision. Near
that point lies a small hill. Adam and Eve
intend to climb it.

              They process along
the dirt road like two muses on Parnassus.
The point at which the city light leaps into
view is their first stop. Adam looks up to

the pseudo-spires, then, farther on toward
the bister light that shines through the smog-filled flats.
He soon looks up at the full moon. Eve takes
a breath of the wind's orange-blossom perfume.
There is a strong east wind that pushes through
the coastal-sage-scrub plain. Oak limbs groan like
arthritic bones. He turns to the small hill.
He sees the large back of a taller hill
beyond it. That hill has short chaparral
and spots where tall pine trees grow. There's a stretch
of tiny, verdant valley through those hills.
The tiny, verdant valley's very well
protected and enclosed. In fact, there's not
a single sign of human life around
except a well-worn path that passes through
an orange grove and lemon trees. This scene
reminds Adam and Eve of other days.

GAIL WHITE

Lost Daughters

They vanish on their way to school.
A love of reading is their crime.
Bound to obey a different rule,

They marry long before their time.
(They may be wives, they may be slaves).
Their parents have no strength to climb

Out of the pits of daughters' graves.
They keep their younger girls inside.
A girl is safe if she behaves

Herself and never seeks a ride
To classes that may fill her head
With words that teach her not to hide

But to respect herself instead.
A daughter mustnn't be a fool.
So many lost, so many dead —
They vanish on their way to school.

RICHARD WIDERKEHR

Ariel Released

His last day on the island, Prospero said
to follow him where sea stacks guard the sea.
Under one arm, he lugged his magic book.
climbing the broken shore. From a high stand
overlooking the island's point, he stared
at the horizon. When he shook his head,
the sea grew wild. I feared he'd never set
me free. Wind stung our faces with fine spray
shaken from basalt caves that clenched and ground
as wave after wave fell on the steep shore.
When had they wished for loss of majesty?
He stood above them on the jutting height
and seemed no different. Nothing changed his gaze.
But all at once, he knelt down and released
his book like breath into the ocean's jaw.
I guessed he thought it was the proper way.
At last, he stood up. Leaning on one leg,
he clutched his sleeve. For the first time, his eyes
were scored with crooked veins. When I looked down,
he told me I was free. I felt the wind
push in around me. Tears came to my eyes.
I asked to walk with him at least to where
the shore line bends, but he said no. Was I
ungrateful to him? Did I condescend?
I hadn't thought to hope he'd set me free.
And so I'm free. Often I think of times
his magic turned the world into a stage,
and I watched by his side, or tricked a fool,
arranged a masque, saw to the tempest, told
him what came next when he forgot. I was
important. Now I often find myself

alone, here on the human shore. The island
is mine. The waves resume their punishment.
I wonder if Prospero's new life is good,
if it's been worth it after all, and if
he left me here on purpose. Caliban,
the monster, hankers for a god to serve
again. He walks, sighing among the trees,
and nothing answers. Sometimes when the night
is cold, I think I might do worse that choose
me for his god. But Prospero's image stays
with me like years. I think of him with head thrust
back and eyes fixed on the sea's flat rim.
For till he unlocked all our bondages,
wasn't my master yearning to be free?

KATHERINE SMITH

Sunflowers

Around the vase of garish store-bought flowers
placed on the table so each yellow face,
foreshortened, bows to students in the hours
we spend in miming their questionable taste,

an Army major, newly civilian, draws
a delicate shadow under transparent petals.
Retired librarians mix their blues with ochre
to hammer sunflowers like coppery metals.

Around the table classmates' foreheads frown.
Their eyebrows raise or dip with every stroke
of brush that carries vision to solid ground.
Meanwhile, obsessed with meaning, I choke

and muddy yellows, wasting half an hour
feeling superior to the tacky vase,
comparing this hideous arrangement of flowers
to fields whose majesty fills my mind with grace.

From retina, nerve, and bone, my errors flow
from brushes, staining the clear water charcoal.
I work, forget the vision of the grandiose,
struggle to capture ordinary gold.

SUSAN MCLEAN

One Death

The art of dying isn't hard to master.
"Just sign this form: Do Not Resuscitate."
It costs the hospice less if she dies faster.

"We'll gladly give her drugs or call a pastor.
We do not cure. We just alleviate."
The art of dying isn't hard to master.

"Infection has set in? That's no disaster.
We don't treat lesions when they suppurate."
It costs the hospice less if she dies faster.

"If she cannot respond to what you've asked her,
think she's at peace. We're here to mitigate."
The art of dying isn't hard to master.

"Recall the pain and nausea that harassed her.
Death is the cure, so why procrastinate?"
It costs the hospice less if she dies faster.

"By now, the days she'd want to face are past her.
We don't prolong. We simply palliate."
The art of dying isn't hard to master.
It costs the hospice less if she dies faster.

TERESE COE

Everness

After Jorge Luis Borges

Only one thing does not exist. Oblivion.
God, who shields the metal, shields the slag
and encodes in his prophetic memory
the moons that were and the moons that are to come.
All of it is there. The worlds of reflections
that between the double twilights of the day
your face has left behind inside the mirrors,
and those that it will leave here once again.
And all of it is part of the diverse
crystal of that memory, the universe;
its corridors are hard and have no end,
and as you pass the doors will close once more;
only on the other side of sundown
will you see the archetypes and splendors.

ROBERT MCNAMARA

For My Wife, Late Summer, Gardening

Summer you chased God's change-up, wicked curves,
through weeks of drought, a nail-biting hour of hail.
You got your hits, sweet corn, tomatoes, kale.
Hard work, well-done. But does that mean *deserved?*

Today you're digging in a lovely compost,
with shovel, hoe and grandkids, giving back
to soil some of its own, burned in the dark
by legions of red wrigglers the kids find *gross.*

We watch with them a puppeteer of air,
spinning a shroud for a still-quivering fly.
Spider will have his supper bye and bye,
Do you think so? Who is to say it's fair, not fair?

The garden's fresh because the garden dies.
You're with us here. Do you see us cry?

CATHERINE CHANDLER

Anthracite

Nothing, short of time, can put them out.
All attempts to quash the blazes fail —
water-dousing, trenches, slurry, grout.
Blue coal bits commingle with the shale.

Nothing to rescue, nothing to reclaim;
so, in a smoldering of suppressed desire,
she marries, but she keeps her maiden name,
her life a burning slag heap. Culm bank fire.

Stuart Jay Silverman

What We See

There she goes, or he, steady as a snail,
a round red drunk leering over a fence.
Night is just around the corner. A trail
of light wanders about the ghastly grass.

The moon whitens. Crickets warm to their work.
Is it that the coming has come to pass,
and meaning soon will break into being?
Nothing of that is what we're seeing.

Wisdom doesn't erupt into the clear.
The moon never wavers inching up the sky,
her round face curding to yellowish whey.

Nothing more. Star glints reliably steer
as, starry-eyed, their hosts did in their day
until their fuel cells coughed up a last sigh.

STUART JAY SILVERMAN

A Brief History of the World in Two Parts

I

Once, Adam, wrestling with a rock,
Saw angels gathered, row on row,
Who told him he and Eve must go.
He looked about him, taking stock,
Then, noticing a gate agape,
Said *exile's almost like escape.*

Whatever goods were left behind,
Out there new vines and fruit trees rose.
Deer, panicked by a footstep, froze.
The garden looked a touch refined,
In retrospect, God less than fair
Who'd left temptation in his care.

In time, the garden wore to myth;
God himself drooped, old and faded.
The sons of Adam raped and raided.
Some made of God a monolith
On which to sacrifice the hearts
Of other sons from other parts.

II

Eve figured there was no percentage
In lingering with Adam gone.
"Thank god," she thought, "the sheep are shorn."
Loading them with woven tentage,
She followed Adam to the wild.
In due course, she produced a child.

In due course, the children she begot,
Begot, in turn, godawful messes,
Which, happily, the priest that blesses
Made holy, blessing on the spot.
For a consideration given,
Sins and sinners both are shriven.

Believing, fearing, made to fall,
Eve learned diplomacy and guile.
She learned a watchful, waiting style,
She learned to fence, and hedge, and stall.
She learned to swallow pride with pain,
And, so, survives, against the grain.

Kim Bridgford

Acquiesce (I)

You have to yield. You have to go along,
And if you don't, you will go anyway.
To acquiesce is to accept a wrong.

That's how the ones in power stay so strong.
They run you over. How about *this way?*
You have to yield. You have to go along.

Yet you don't feel so good when the forked tongue
Spits you out. One elbow up, you weigh
The reason why to acquiesce is wrong:

Because your self-respect is twisted, wrung.
At work, in bed, in bars, in trains, to say
You have to yield, you have to go along,

Will kill you in the short- and longer run.
Regret and conscience wake you up at 3:00.
You acquiesced. You knew that it was wrong.

You notice that the men you move among
Don't see you as you are. All that they see
Is someone who must yield, must go along.
To acquiesce is to accept a wrong.

Stephen Gibson

The Tate Gallery Ophelia

She floated in Millais's icy bath tub, not a river.
High as a kite, Elizabeth Siddal, dressed
in heavy brocade posing as Ophelia,
didn't feel anything. The artist
had spent the summer

at the Hogsmill River painting its banks of flowers.
That winter, he was filling her in. He confessed —
at her drug overdose inquest a decade later —
the heat lamps went out; he didn't notice.
In the icy bath tub

Lizzie got cold and later developed pneumonia.
Millais testified at the dead model's inquest
he only noticed her singing like Ophelia
in the icy bath tub.

STEPHEN GIBSON

Ophelia

If she could see the future, would it matter?
Change things? She might say it would.
Cassandra could shout it, and she wouldn't believe her.

There she is, Elizabeth Siddal, twenty-two, as Ophelia
floating down a river like a piece of wood —
if she could see the future, would it matter?

It's a bath tub — and not the Hogsmill River
where tourists come to stand where Millais stood.
Cassandra could shout it, and she wouldn't believe her.

She'll overdose in ten years — after a stillborn daughter
and an unfaithful husband who'll say he did all he could.
If she could see the future, would it matter?

Tourists take the tube to the Tate to see *Ophelia* —
asked if they could change the future, most would.
Cassandra could shout it, and no one would believe her.

The heat lamps are out: she doesn't feel the icy water
because she's young, high on laudanum, and life is good.
If she could see the future, would it matter?
Cassandra could shout it, and she wouldn't believe her.

BURT MYERS

Drought

In this city of idiot grins, it's always raining.
A smattering of birds feather to confetti
over the shabby rowhouses straining
against the horizon. "Is it April already?"

asks my imagined companion. I'm shivering.
We walk together till the streets narrow,
ignoring the refuse in our path, piss rivering
the gutters, into some unfamiliar borough.

I try to meet her eye, blunder into a puddle
and fall. She unveils an umbrella. I take her
hand and lean into the gravity of her shadow.
She lifts me up, dry in her marigold slicker.

MICHAEL SHEWMAKER

The Neighbors Upstairs

They only stirred at night while we were sleeping.
In a small space that must have mirrored ours,
they moved freely between the muted hours —
my father's snoring and my mother's weeping.
Like the tired gods that pace above this city —
abolished and forgotten by the hand
that shaped them, prodigals who understand
the gravity of loss — they showed no pity
for those who slept beneath them.
                      From the vent,
a tremolo of words — though indistinct,
distorted by the duct, yet somehow linked
to longing — kept me up with their intent.

But now that I am older, torn by choices,
it's difficult to sleep without their voices.

MICHAEL SHEWMAKER

The Illusionist

Without the usual work of wands,
she dazzles solely with her hands.

The coin behind your ear is gone.
Her turtledoves have turned to stone.

She plucks the rose from her corsage,
your ring tucked in its petaled cage.

She knows your card. She levitates.
The coin appears in duplicates.

And though she makes a show of it —
the scripted struggle, the long wait —

no locks or chains are sound enough
to bind her to this stage. And though

you know the limits of the eye,
her sleight of hand, the hidden lie,

you choose to see as through a sieve.
You still applaud. You still believe.

MICHAEL SHEWMAKER

School Bus Graveyard

Their carcasses decay beneath the weather.
Honeysuckle crowds the wheel wells, snakes
around their sagging axles. The sun strips
their paint and splits the leather.
                                    What wrecks
are these that once were counted on? Dead ships
on a dry sea? At evening, when I pass,
I see small hands and faces in the glass.

CODY WALKER

This is the Neighbor Kid Who Killed the Cat

This is the neighbor kid who killed the cat.
This is your father who thinks like that.
This is your mother who throws up her hands.
This is the algorithm that misunderstands.

This is the jackhammer that hates the rock.
This is the safety at war with the Glock.
This is your lab partner, stockpiling Xanax.
This is your captain — watch as he panics.

This is your nightmare, bright as day.
This is your police scanner. What will it say?
These are your boots to wipe on the mat.
Mark down your casualties. Hang up your hat.

CODY WALKER

We Hated Our Lives

We hated our lives so we dug up the fern
And gassed the azaleas and emptied the urn

And severed our fingers and salted our toes
Which caused us to stumble, but that's how it goes

We jetted to India, jetted to Spain
We scattered our clothes in the wind and the rain

We gobbled the photos and drank all the ink
And tortured a Gabonese charlatan shrink

And who would be waiting, upon our return?
Our kids, at our doorstep, expressing concern

CODY WALKER

Conditional

If worker bees would work for free,
We'd chance a honeymoon;
And you'd let go that thing I said
Yesterday afternoon.

The sun would quickstep in the sky,
March would yield to June,
And you'd let go that thing I said
Yesterday afternoon.

ANNA LENA PHILLIPS BELL

Ornament

Make me down a pallet on your floor.
— Mississippi John Hurt

Is mine a gaudy God,
one of bobbins, pins?
Are you of salt and sod
or mine, a gaudy God
who — fingers thimble-shod,
baubled, bezelled, — begins —
be mine, a gaudy God,
one of bobbins, pins.

Are you of salt and sod,
a fish, an element?
Do leaves fall where you've trod —
are you of salt and sod
and span of milkweed pod,
seed-sailing filament?
Are you of salt and sod,
a fish, an element?

Do leaves fall where you've trod?
Do you call the forest yours,
make down a meadow bed?
Do leaves fall where you've trod,
your hands brush goldenrod,
your lips, with deer, meet pears?
Do leaves fall where you've trod?
Is all the forest yours?

Make down a meadow bed.
Make me your only own.
Be mine, a gaudy God —
make down a meadow bed
with moss beneath your head,
soft sheets to slumber on.
Make down a meadow bed;
make me your own.

Anna Lena Phillips Bell

Bonaparte Crossing the Rhine

When he had gone I sat and played alone,
remembering how I'd told him "Go to hell"
and feeling dismal. Who knew I'd recall
that melody? It marched in slow and fine
and brought back not his body but the sound
of notes we'd played, an echo, rise, and swell
that swept on up the fretboard as I fell
in love — with him? I must've lost my mind.
I thought I'd take the player, would as soon
sin as settle for less. But memory serves
me well, suggests another, better plan:
it holds the music — never mind the man —
and I've been playing long enough to prove
that this arrangement's fine. I'll keep the tune.

ANNA LENA PHILLIPS BELL

Green Man

He will not subside,   won't slip into leaf-mold;
he lived in the woods   where my father found him:
a weathered plank   with waiting sockets.
He carried him home   and carved the cedar:
a narrow nose   nestled in red crest
lichen, lips   like his own, and scuppernong
beard; bronze ivy   to crown his brows.
Last, he split walnuts   and wedged each half
into its hollow,   hallowed his face
with cool creek water,   and called him whole.
Then, as he'd promised,   he posted him north.
Dry moss crackled   in the bubble mailer;
wide eyes emerged   to watch me while
I made him a place   in my winter house
and bade him rest.   Now, as I breathe,
a verdant current   fills craven air:
he exhales, his mouth   speaks moss, makes leaf.

Acknowledgments

ANNA LENA PHILLIPS BELL. "Ornament," "Bonaparte Crossing the Rhine," and "Green Man" are from *Ornament*. Copyright 2017. Reprinted with permission of the author and University of North Texas Press.

MICHAEL SHEWMAKER. "The Neighbors Upstairs," "The Illusionist," and "School Bus Graveyard" are from *Penumbra*. Copyright 2017. Reprinted with permission of the author and Ohio University Press.

CODY WALKER. "This is the Neighbor Kid Who Killed the Cat," "We Hated Our Lives," and "Conditional" are from *The Self-Styled No-Child*. Copyright 2016. Reprinted with permission of the author and The Waywiser Press.

CONTRIBUTORS

CHAD ABUSHANAB's poems have appeared or are forthcoming in *The Hopkins Review*, *32 Poems*, *Unsplendid*, *The Raintown Review*, and others. He is a doctoral student in literature and creative writing at Texas Tech University, and the poetry editor of *Arcadia*.

ALLISON ADAIR's recent poems appear or are forthcoming in *American Poetry Review*, *Best New Poets 2015*, *Boston Review*, *Los Angeles Review*, *Mid-American Review*, and *Mississippi Review*, among other journals. Winner of the Fall 2015 Orlando Prize and the 2014 Fineline Competition, Adair teaches at Boston College and Grub Street.

MIKE ALEXANDER, having emigrated from North Jersey to Southeast Texas during the last fin de siècle, continues to run readings and publishes in several magazines. His first book, *Retrograde*, was published in 2013. He also has worked on *Lyric*, Mutabilis Press, and *Public Poetry*.

GILBERT ALLEN's most recent books are *The Final Days of Great American Shopping* and *Catma*. Some of his newest work appears in *Kestrel*, *New Verse News*, *Poetry Daily*, *The Southern Review*, and *Tampa Review*. He lives in upstate South Carolina with his wife, Barbara.

TONY BARNSTONE teaches at Whittier College and is the author of 18 books and a music CD. His books of poetry include *Pulp Sonnets*; *Beast in the Apartment*; *Tongue of War: From Pearl Harbor to Nagasaki*; *The Golem of Los Angeles*; *Sad Jazz: Sonnets*; and *Impure*. He is also a distinguished translator of Chinese literature. His awards include the Poets' Prize, Strokestown International, Pushcart, John Ciardi Prize, Benjamin Saltman Award, and fellowships from the NEA, NEH, and California Arts Council.

ANNA LENA PHILLIPS BELL's poems have appeared in the *Southern Review*, *32 Poems*, and *Poetry International*. The recipient of an NC Arts Council Fellowship, she teaches at UNC Wilmington and is editor of *Ecotone*. She lives with her family near the Cape Fear River.

STEPHEN BLUESTONE lives in Brooklyn, NY, and has won The Thomas Merton Prize and the Greensboro Prize, among others.

Previous books of poetry include *The Laughing Monkeys of Gravity* and *The Flagrant Dead* (Mercer University Press). *The Painted Clock*, a new volume, is forthcoming. His work has appeared in *Poetry*, *The Sewanee Review*, *Boston Review*, and other journals.

BRUCE BOND is the author of fifteen books including, most recently, *For the Lost Cathedral* (LSU, 2015), *The Other Sky* (Etruscan, 2015), and *Immanent Distance: Poetry and the Metaphysics of the Near at Hand* (University of Michigan Press, 2015). Four of his books are forthcoming: *Black Anthem* (Tampa Review Prize, University of Tampa Press), *Gold Bee* (Crab Orchard Open Competition Award, SIU Press), *Sacrum* (Four Way Books), and *Blackout Starlight: New and Selected Poems* (L.E. Phillabaum Award, LSU). He is Regents Professor at University of North Texas.

KIM BRIDGFORD is the director of Poetry by the Sea: A Global Conference, and the curator of the Poetry by the Sea Reading Series at the Pennsylvania Academy of the Fine Arts in Center City, Philadelphia. Bridgford is the editor of *Mezzo Cammin*, and the founder of The Mezzo Cammin Women Poets Timeline Project. The author of nine books of poetry, including the recent *Human Interest*, she is the recipient of grants from the NEA and the Ucross Foundation.

DAN CAMPION's poems have appeared previously in *Measure* and in other magazines, including *Able Muse*, *Blue Unicorn*, *Ekphrasis*, *Light*, *The Midwest Quarterly*, *The North American Review*, *Poetry*, *Rolling Stone*, and *Shenandoah*, and in anthologies, including *Amethyst and Agate: Poems of Lake Superior* (Holy Cow! Press, 2015).

CATHERINE CHANDLER is the author of *The Frangible Hour*, winner of the 2016 Richard Wilbur Award (University of Evansville Press, 2016). Other books include *Lines of Flight* (Able Muse Press), shortlisted for the Poets' Prize; *Glad and Sorry Seasons* (Biblioasis); *This Sweet Order* (White Violet Press); and two chapbooks.

TERESE COE's poems and translations have appeared in *Measure*, *Threepenny Review*, *Poetry*, *New American Writing*, *Ploughshares*, *Alaska Quarterly Review*, *The Cincinnati Review*, and the *TLS*. Her latest collection of poems, *Shot Silk*, was published by Kelsay Books.

PETER COOLEY has published nine books, eight of them with

Carnegie Mellon. Cooley's most recent book, which deals with Hurricane Katrina, is *Night Bus to the Afterlife*. His work has appeared in *The New Yorker, The Atlantic, The Nation, The New Republic,* and in over one hundred anthologies.

CAROL FRITH, co-editor of *Ekphrasis,* has chapbooks from Bacchae Press, Finishing Line, Rattlesnake Press, Medicinal Purposes, Palanquin Press, and Gribble Press. Her first full-length collection was released in 2010 from David Robert Books. Her poems have appeared in *Measure, Atlanta Review, Seattle Review, Midwest Quarterly, POEM, The Formalist, Rattle, Smartish Pace, Rhino, Poetry Kanto,* and elsewhere.

MOIRA EGAN lives in Rome, and when she is not teaching or translating, she can be found sniffing perfumes and looking at paintings, and then writing ekphrastic poems based on those experiences.

STEPHEN GIBSON is the author of five poetry collections: *Rorschach Art Too* (West Chester University), *Paradise* (University of Arkansas Press), *Frescoes* (Lost Horse Press), *Masaccio's Expulsion* (MARGIE/ IntuiT House) and *Rorschach Art* (Red Hen). New work appears in *American Arts Quarterly, Louisiana Literature, River Styx, The Sewanee Review, Shenandoah, Southwest Review, The Yale Review,* and others.

BILL GLOSE is a former paratrooper and author of three poetry collections, including *Half a Man,* whose poems arise from his experiences as a combat platoon leader in the Gulf War. His poems have appeared in numerous journals, including *The Missouri Review, Narrative Magazine, Poet Lore,* and *Atlanta Review.*

JAMES HAINES lives in Lawrence, Kansas. His poems have appeared most recently in *Spank the Carp, Inscape, Naugatuck River Review, Blue Island Review,* and *The Evening Street Review.* Poems are forthcoming in *Little Balkans Review.* He is a woodworker and is retired from a career in law, business, and teaching.

JEFF HARDIN is the author of four collections of poetry, most recently *Notes for a Praise Book, Restoring the Narrative,* and *Small Revolution.* Recent and forthcoming poems appear in *The Southern Review, Southwest Review, Birmingham Poetry Review, IthacaLit, The Laurel Review, New American Writing, Tupelo Quarterly,* and elsewhere.

JEFF HOLT is a Licensed Professional Counselor from Dallas, Texas. He has recently published poetry in *Angle* and has previously published poetry in *Antiphon Poetry Magazine*, *String Poet*, *The Nervous Breakdown*, and various other journals and anthologies. In 2012, White Violet Press published Jeff's first book, *The Harvest*.

SIMON HUNT was born in Rhodesia (now Zimbabwe) and raised in England and the United States. His poems have appeared or are forthcoming in *Homestead Review*, *Light Quarterly*, *The Raintown Review*, *The Seventh Quarry*, *The Sewanee Review*, and other journals.

ROB JACKSON has recent poems published in *Southwest Review*, *Boston Literary Magazine*, *Southern California Review*, *The Lyric*, *Light*, and *Avocet*. He has two books of children's poetry with the Highlights publishing group and has read his poetry on National Public Radio. He is also an environmental scientist and climate change expert at Stanford.

KATHRYN JACOBS is professor at Texas A & M – C and editor of *The Road Not Taken: A Journal of Formal Poetry*. Her fifth volume of poetry, *Wedged Elephant*, was published last year by Kelsay Books. She also has a book from University Press of Florida, *Marriage Contracts From Chaucer to the Renaissance Stage*. Her poems appear in *Measure*, *Acumen*, *Raintown Review*, and *Wordgathering*, among others.

MARK JARMAN's most recent collections of poetry are *Bone Fires: New and Selected Poems* (Sarabande Books, 2011) and *The Heronry* (Sarabande Books, 2017). He is Centennial Professor of English at Vanderbilt University.

A.M. JUSTER is a three-time winner of the Howard Nemerov Sonnet Award whose work has appeared in *Poetry*, *Paris Review*, *Rattle*, *Hudson Review*, and many other journals. His eighth book, *The Elegies of Maximianus*, will be released by the University of Pennsylvania Press in early 2018.

DAVID LANDRUM has published poetry in many journals and magazines, most recently in *Misty Mountain Review*, *Think*, *The Orchards*, *Three Drops from a Cauldron*, and *The Dark Ones*. He teaches English at Grand Valley State University in Allendale, Michigan.

QUINCY R. LEHR writes poems. Sometimes. They appear in

books. Periodically. He does readings. Occasionally.

CHARLES MARTIN's most recent book of poems is *Signs & Wonders* (Johns Hopkins University Press, 2011). His verse translation of the *Metamorphoses* of Ovid received the Harold Morton Landon Award from the Academy of American Poets in 2004. In 2005, he received an Award for Literature from the American Academy of Arts and Letters. His most recent book is a collaborative translation (with Sanscrit scholar Gavin Flood,) of the *Bhagavad Gita*, published by W.W. Norton in 2012.

ASHLEY ANNA MCHUGH's debut poetry collection, *Into These Knots*, was the 2010 winner of The New Criterion Poetry Prize. *Become All Flame*, a limited-edition chapbook of her poetry, was published by LATR Editions. She was the 2009 winner of the Morton Marr Poetry Prize, and her poems have appeared in *Nimrod*, *The New Criterion*, *The Journal*, and *The Hopkins Review*, among other venues.

SUSAN MCLEAN is an English professor at Southwest Minnesota State University. Her books include *The Best Disguise* and *The Whetstone Misses the Knife* and and translations of Martial, *Selected Epigrams*. Her poems and translations have recently appeared in *The Classical Outlook*, *Light*, and *Lighten Up Online*.

ROBERT MCNAMARA has published three books of poetry, and over the last thirty years his poems have appeared widely in journals and anthologies. His most recent book, *Incomplete Strangers*, was featured in *Measure*, Volume VIII, Issue 1 (2013).

LESLIE MONSOUR is the author of *The Alarming Beauty of the Sky* and *The House Sitter*. Her work has been featured on several broadcasts of NPR's "Writer's Almanac" and published in various journals, including *Poetry*, *The Dark Horse*, *Able Muse*, *American Arts Quarterly*, and *Light*. She has received four Pushcart Prize nominations and an NEA fellowship.

BURT MYERS works as an art director in upstate New York. His poems have appeared in *The Hopkins Review*, *The Birmingham Poetry Review*, *Tar River Poetry*, and others.

STEPHEN PALOS is from Lexington, KY. He received his BA in English from the Ohio State University and his MFA in creative writing from the University of Michigan. His work has appeared in the *Allegheny Review* and *Pluck! Journal* and is forthcoming in *Able Muse* and the *Raintown Review*.

BILLY REYNOLDS' poems have been published in *32 Poems*, *Chattahoochee Review*, *Iron Horse Literary Review*, *Sewanee Theological Review*, and *Zone 3*, among others. Currently, he lives in Kalamazoo, Michigan.

JOHN RIDLAND's translation of *Sir Gawain and the Green Knight* (Able Muse Press, 2016) is being followed by a translation of the same Middle English poet's *Pearl*. Other work has been published or accepted in *Askew*, *Miramar*, and *Per Contra*.

THOM SATTERLEE's *Burning Wyclif* was a 2007 American Library Association Notable Book and a Finalist for the L.A. Times Book Prize in poetry. He lives in Marion, Indiana.

STEPHEN SCAER lives in Nashua, NH, and is a special education teacher with poems published in *Highlights*, *First Things*, *Cricket*, and *National Review*. His collection of verse, *Pumpkin Chucking*, is available from Able Muse Press.

MAE SCANLAN's humorous verse has appeared in books, magazines, newspapers, and online publications in both the U.S. and Great Britain. She also writes songs and song parodies for various events in the Washington, D.C. area, where she and her husband live.

ROBERT SCHECHTER has published poems in *The Evansville Review*, *Light Quarterly*, *The Raintown Review*, *The Washington Post*, *The Everyman* "Villanelles" anthology, *The Spectator*, and *Highlights for Children*, among other places.

ROY SCHEELE published a chapbook of sonnets, *The Sledders*, in January 2016; one poem from that collection, "In Possession (Minnesota)," recently appeared in Ted Kooser's column "American Life in Poetry." Scheele also has two ekphrastic sonnets forthcoming in *ArtMove*, and several other poems will appear in *Nebraska Poetry: A Sesquicentennial Anthology, 1867-2017* from Stephen F. Austin State University Press.

MICHAEL SHEWMAKER is a Jones Lecturer in poetry at Stanford

University. His first collection of poems, *Penumbra*, is the recent winner of the Hollis Summers Poetry Prize (Ohio UP, 2017). A former Wallace Stegner Fellow, his poems appear or are forthcoming in *Yale Review*, *Virginia Quarterly Review*, *Poetry Daily*, *Parnassus*, *Oxford American*, *New Criterion*, *Narrative*, *Hopkins Review*, *Columbia*, and other literary journals and anthologies. He lives in the San Francisco Bay Area with his wife, Emily.

STUART JAY SILVERMAN divides his life between homes in Chicago, IL, and Hot Springs, AR. He writes traditional poetry in the belief that Parnassus has room for meter and rhyme in its capacious mansion, and he tries to create worlds and experiences which go beyond the mere expression of feeling.

KATHERINE SMITH's work has been published in *Missouri Review*, *Cincinnati Review*, *Ploughshares*, *Gargoyle*, *The Journal of the Motherhood Initiative*, *Poetry*, *Shenandoah*, and *The Southern Review*. She is the author of *Argument by Design* and *Woman Alone on the Mountain*.

SOFIA M. STARNES, Virginia's Poet Laureate from 2012 to 2014, is the author of five poetry collections and editor of two poetry anthologies. Her first full-length collection, *A Commerce of Moments*, was named Honor Book by the Library of Virginia in the year of its publication. She serves as Poetry Editor and Poetry Book Review Editor of *The Anglican Theological Review*.

DOLORES STEWART's poems have appeared in *The American Scholar*, *Atlanta Review*, *The Beloit Poetry Journal*, *California Quarterly*, *Chicago Review*, and other journals. Two collections of her poems, *Doors to the Universe* and *The Nature of Things*, have been published by Bellowing Ark Press.

N.S. THOMPSON is a British poet and translator and non-fiction editor for *Able Muse*. Recently he co-edited and contributed to *A Modern Don Juan: Cantos for These Times by Divers Hands* (Five Leaves, 2014), where fifteen poets bring Byron's hero into the 21st century.

HERB WAHLSTEEN was a finalist in the Yale Series of Younger Poets contest and has published poems in *Long Island Quarterly*, *Great South Bay Magazine*, *The Lyric*, *Paumanok Interwoven*, *Suffolk County Poetry Review*, *Bards Annual*, *Form Quarterly*, *13 Days of Halloween*, and *String*.

CODY WALKER is the author of *Shuffle and Breakdown* (Waywiser Press, 2008) and the co-editor of *Alive the Center: Contemporary Poems from the Pacific Northwest* (Ooligan Press, 2013). His poems have appeared in *The Yale Review, Parnassus, Slate, Poetry Northwest, The Hecht Prize Anthology*, and *The Best American Poetry* (2007 and 2015); his essays have appeared online in *The New Yorker* and *The Kenyon Review*. He lives with his family in Ann Arbor, where he teaches English at the University of Michigan.

GAIL WHITE is a contributing editor of *Light* and a two-time winner of the Howard Nemerov Sonnet Award. Her latest book, *Asperity Street*, was published in 2015 by Able Muse Press. She lives in Breaux Bridge, Louisiana.

RICHARD WIDERKEHR has two book-length collections of poems: *The Way Home* (Plain View Press) and *Her Story of Fire* (Egress Studio Press). Recent work has appeared in *Rattle, Floating Bridge Review, Cirque, Penumbra, Clay Bird Review*, and *Salt River Review*. He is a poetry editor for *Shark Reef Review*.

JAMES MATTHEW WILSON is Associate Professor of Religion and Literature at Villanova University. He has published six books, including, *Some Permanent Things*, and the controversial critical study, *The Fortunes of Poetry in an Age of Unmaking*.

THE 2017 X.J. KENNEDY PARODY AWARD

$500 Prize

Final Judge: Eric McHenry

Deadline: September 30, 2017

1)   Submissions must be original, unpublished parodies of famous poems of any length and subject matter.

2)   Parodies must be metrical (accentual-syllabic or accentual), though the original poem may be free verse.

3)   Author's name, address, phone number, e-mail address, and name of poem being parodied should by typed on each entry.

4)   Final judge for the 2017 contest will be Eric McHenry. The winning poem and severals runners-up will be published in a 2018 issue of *Measure*.

5)   Send up to three poems in one envelepe (or in one MS Word file via our electronic submission system). Entry fee: $10 per three poems, check payable to "Measure Press." Writers may enter as many times as they'd like, but each group of three poems must by accompanied by a $10 fee.

6)   Entries must be sent to the address below and postmarked no later than September 30, 2017. Enclose an SASE if you would like to be notified of the contest results. Entries cannot be returned.

Measure Parody Award
Department of Creative Writing
1800 Lincoln Avenue
Evansville, IN 47722

Or

http://measure press.com/measure

Please note: These are the complee guidelines. Thank you.

THE 2017 HOWARD NEMEROV SONNET AWARD

$1000 Prize

Final Judge: Dana Gioia

Deadline: November 15, 2017

1)   Sonnets must be original and unpublished. No translations. Writers may enter up to twelve sonnets. Sonnet sequences are acceptable, but each sonnet will be considered individually. Entry fee: $3 per sonnet, checks payable to **"The Formalist."** Entry fees from outside the U.S. must be paid in cash — U.S. dollars — or by a check drawn on a U.S. bank. Author's name, address, phone number, and e-mail address should be typed on the ***back*** of each entry.

2)   Final Judge for the 2017 competition will be Dana Gioia. The winning poem and eleven finalist poems will be published in a 2018 issue of *Measure: A Review of Formal Poetry*.

3)   Entries must be sent to the address below and postmarked no later than November 15, 2017. The winner and finalist poems will be announced on Eratosphere in January. Enclose an SASE if you would like to be notified of the contest results. Entries cannot be returned.

Howard Nemerov Sonnet Award
The Formalist
21 Osborne Terrace
Wayne, NJ 07470

CPSIA information can be obtained
at www.ICGtesting.com
Printed in the USA
FSOW01n1641260917
39175FS